W9-CER-058

Adoption

Look for these and other books in the Lucent Overview Series:

Adoption

by Stephen Currie

LUCENT
BOOKS

LUCENT *Overview Series*

LUCENT *Overview Series*

Library of Congress Cataloging-in-Publication Data

Currie, Stephen, 1960–
    Adoption / by Stephen Currie.
       p. cm. — (Lucent overview series)
    Includes bibliographical references and index.
    Summary: Discusses issues related to adoption, including parental rights, racial mixing, international adopting, and privacy concerns.
    ISBN 1-56006-183-9 (alk. paper)
    1. Adoption—Juvenile literature. [1. Adoption.] I. Title.
II. Series.
  HV875.C86 1997
  362.7'34—dc20   96-34145
                                            CIP
                                            AC

Copyright © 1997 by Lucent Books, Inc.
P.O. Box 289011, San Diego, CA 92198-9011
Printed in the U.S.A.

Contents

Introduction

A HUNDRED AND FIFTY years ago, adoption as we know it did not exist. Adoption in those days usually meant one of two things: a child moved in with relatives, or a child lived with an unrelated family in exchange for work. In neither case would the adults become the child's legal parents. Such adoptions were often temporary, and there was no expectation that the adopted child would be treated like the new family's biological children.

Over time, however, adoption became a more and more formal arrangement, increasingly intended to safeguard the interests of the child. By the end of the nineteenth century, most states required that various legal steps be taken before an adoption could proceed. These included an official surrender by the birth parents, issuance of an adoption decree by a judge, and an investigation to make sure the new parents were fit to care for a child. By World War II, adoptions were expected to be permanent, and the adopted child became an equal member of the family both legally and morally. Indeed, for many years the fact of a child's adoption was rarely revealed to the rest of the world—or even to the child.

The adoption controversies discussed in this book are not those of 150 years ago, when a burning question might have been whether it was possible to treat an adopted child as a true member of the family. They are not the same as those of 30 years ago, when a heated topic might have been whether it was ethical to tell a child that he or she was adopted. Presumably, 50 years from now society will be wrestling with adoption issues we cannot anticipate.

But the biggest controversies, today as well as in the past, have always touched on fundamental issues beyond those of adoption itself.

A well-publicized Pennsylvania case resulted when one family returned its adopted son to the agency that had handled the adoption. The child had been impossible to manage, the parents said. An inquiry revealed that the agency knew the child had been severely abused by his biological parents before being freed for adoption, but had decided not to tell the boy's new family the facts of his background. The agency reasoned that the boy might never be adopted if the truth were known. The family was furious and sued the agency for damages. Some observers approve of such lawsuits; an adoption agency, they argue, is subject

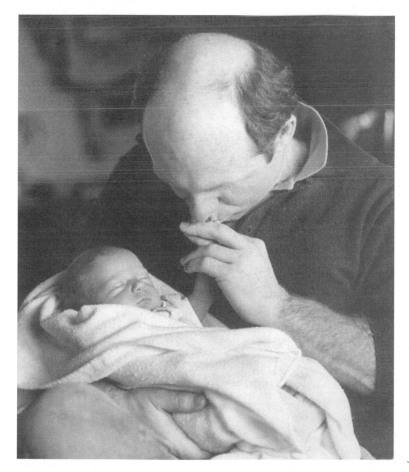

A father gently kisses the hand of his newly adopted son. Today, much of the controversy surrounding adoption centers on what constitutes a family.

A roadside billboard boldly advertises an adoption agency's services. Many people criticize the adoption process for resembling a business transaction and failing to address ethical and moral issues.

to the same laws and ethics as any other business, and this agency's act was the equivalent of a hardware store's knowingly selling a customer a leaky faucet. But others are appalled. "This is not a question of damaged goods," says one law professor. Parents, these advocates argue, make a commitment to be responsible for a child no matter what. Even if an agency behaves inappropriately, they maintain, the parents cannot simply return the child. In fact, the issue is only partly over adoption; it is also a debate about ethics, about the permanence of family bonds, and about the degree to which acquiring a baby should resemble a business transaction.

The adoption controversies in this book, then, have to do with the way people see the world. Adoption is more than a legal procedure; it concerns questions of ethics, morality, and family structure. The questions raised in this book are answered in different ways by people whose images of society are fundamentally quite different. Debates about the future of adoption are actually debates about the future of society.

1

Fathers' Rights

In 1991, A BABY GIRL was born in Cedar Rapids, Iowa. No one knew it at the time, but the girl would become one of the most famous people in America before the age of three. Known only as Baby Girl Clausen when she was born, she was soon to be at the center of one of the fiercest adoption battles ever—a controversy over the rights of biological fathers.

Baby Girl Clausen was born on February 8. On February 10, her biological mother, Cara Clausen, signed papers to release the child for adoption. Clausen's boyfriend, whom she listed as the biological father, had no interest in raising the baby, and he signed the papers as well. Meanwhile, a Michigan couple, Jan and Roberta DeBoer, began the necessary arrangements to adopt the child. A week after Baby Girl Clausen was born, the DeBoers arrived in Cedar Rapids to claim her.

On February 25, an Iowa court officially terminated Clausen's rights to the baby. The DeBoers took the child back home to Michigan and named her Jessica. It would be a few months before the adoption could be ruled final, but so far, everything seemed to be going according to plan.

There was only one problem. Cara Clausen had not told the truth. The baby's biological father was not her current boyfriend. Instead, he was her former boyfriend, a man named Dan Schmidt. Schmidt and Clausen had broken up several months before, and Schmidt had not known that Clausen was pregnant. Soon after the DeBoers returned to Michigan, however, Clausen told Schmidt what had

Baby Jessica, shown here with her adoptive parents Jan and Roberta DeBoer, became the center of a fierce custody struggle between her biological father and the DeBoers.

happened. Schmidt decided he wanted the little girl, and during the second week of March, he petitioned the court for custody of the baby.

But the DeBoers decided to fight to keep the child. They thought it was possible that Schmidt was not actually the father. They also suspected he might lose interest if the case took more than a few weeks to resolve. Even when blood tests proved that Schmidt was, indeed, the biological father, the DeBoers did not back down. By then, Jessica had been living with them for six months—nearly her whole life.

In search of the "real" parents

Six months is a long time in an infant's life, but it was only the beginning of a dispute that would last for almost two more years. The case went to courts in both Iowa and Michigan. The DeBoers pointed to the amount of time the baby had been living with them, insisting it would be traumatic for her to move away from them. They also brought up the fact that Schmidt had been a less than ideal father to his two older children; in fact, he had showed very little interest in supporting them either emotionally or financially. Under the circumstances, they argued, the baby was better off with them.

Schmidt, who married Clausen during the legal proceedings, argued that the child could not be taken from him without his permission. He pointed out that he had never signed any forms releasing the baby. As far as he was concerned, Jessica belonged with her own "flesh and blood"—that is, her biological parents. At the end of July 1993, the legal system agreed with him. Jessica DeBoer, age two and a half, moved from Michigan to Iowa and became Anna Schmidt.

The case involved many issues, but the central question was what rights a biological father actually had. The law in Iowa was quite clear. As long as Dan Schmidt had not signed away his rights or "abandoned" the child, the baby was his. The DeBoers' argument that they would be better parents was never considered; by Iowa law, in fact, it could not be. One Iowa judge wrote that he would like to decide the case based on the child's best interest. He called the DeBoers "exemplary" parents, but maintained that the law forced him to look only at whether Dan Schmidt had been treated fairly. And clearly, he concluded, Schmidt had not.

The Baby Jessica case was a media sensation. Magazines and newspapers plastered photos of all four "parents" across their pages. Judges received hundreds of letters a day regarding the case. Politicians got into the act, too: Two Iowa congressmen came out in public support of the DeBoers. Polling organizations conducted

Dan and Cara Schmidt exit a courtroom during the highly publicized Baby Jessica custody case. The case, which involved many issues, was unique in its focus on the rights of the biological father.

nationwide surveys to find out which side Americans favored, and Hollywood studios negotiated for movie rights to the story.

Mixed public response

Reaction to the decision was huge, as well. Some organizations and observers cheered the ruling; one activist argued that biological ties are so strong that children are better off with biological parents under almost any circumstances. Others felt that Schmidt should not have to be deprived of his child because of a lie told by someone else. If Clausen had named him as the father from the beginning, they pointed out, he could have blocked the adoption from the start, before the DeBoers even saw the baby.

Many agreed with this argument. Carole Anderson, representing an anti-adoption group called Concerned United Birthparents, criticized the DeBoers for trying to hang on to the child so long when the odds were so heavily against them. "It is in the best interests of children to be with their

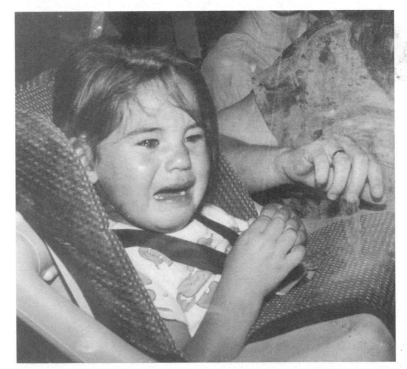

A forlorn Baby Jessica cries as she leaves her adoptive parents in 1993 to begin a new life with her biological parents. The court decision in favor of Baby Jessica's biological father drew mixed reactions from the public.

[biological] families," she argued as the case dragged on, "unless for some reason the family is inadequate." Since no one ever demonstrated that Schmidt was "inadequate," Anderson believed the choice was simple. She blamed the De-Boers for dragging out legal proceedings to "obtain a child who never needed them and will never be wholly theirs." Psychotherapist and author Annette Baran agreed. The DeBoers "managed to pervert the whole issue of best interests of the child," she said.

But others were appalled by the ruling. According to one poll, fewer than 10 percent of Americans supported the Schmidts. Many were dismayed by the notion that the baby somehow "belonged" to the biological parents. "Apparently, adult property rights supersede what's best for the child," complained Susan Freivalds, the executive director of Adoptive Families of America. Anna/Jessica, she pointed out, was not a piece of property but a human being with psychological needs, including the need to stay with the only family she had ever known. "It's outrageous to say that the only issue . . . is whether Dan Schmidt's rights were appropriately terminated," agreed adoption advocate Elizabeth Bartholet. The *New York Times* editorialized that courts ought to take children's rights into account, even if that means sometimes denying custody to biological parents. And a national magazine ran an opinion piece under the title "Baby Jessica Decision: Why the Court Was Wrong."

The issue of fathers' rights did not go away after the Baby Jessica case. If anything, the questions became even more complicated. The DeBoers had never been able to finalize their adoption, so the baby was never legally theirs. But in Illinois in 1995, the courts took the Baby Jessica decision one step further.

Jan and Roberta DeBoer attend a prayer vigil after losing their two-year legal battle to remain Jessica's parents.

Baby Richard

The infant known as Baby Richard was placed for adoption by his mother just after his birth. The mother stated that the father was unknown. According to Illinois law, a biological father had only thirty days to contest adoption proceedings; after that, he forfeited all rights to the child. In thirty days, no father had surfaced for Baby Richard, and the adoptive parents thought they were home free. But when Richard was not quite three months old, a biological father did appear. His name was Otakar Kirchner, and he sued for custody, saying that the mother had lied and told him the baby was dead.

Attorneys for the adoptive couple argued that Kirchner had missed the deadline, but Kirchner went to court to block the adoption anyway. He pointed out that he had shown an interest in the baby as soon as he learned of its existence. Moreover, he argued, he should not be penalized because of a lie told by someone else. The first court decisions, however, went against Kirchner. Baby Richard was formally adopted.

But the case was not over. Kirchner appealed the initial ruling, and when Baby Richard was three and a half, the case came before the Illinois Supreme Court, which reversed the earlier decision. "If this case is a tragedy," wrote Justice James H. Heiple, "then that tragedy is the wrongful breakup of a natural family." The court nullified the adoption and awarded custody to Kirchner. Heiple said he was sorry to take the child away from the couple who had raised him since birth, but predicted that Richard would "get over it quickly."

Again, the decision was enormously controversial. The governor of Illinois called it "a travesty," and dozens of irate citizens called radio talk shows to complain. "How can an old man in a black robe tear a family apart like this?" one caller asked. Kirchner justified the decision. "Adoptive parents can replace the kid," he said. "For biological parents, it's not so easy. Your own kid is your own kid." Many other advocates agreed. Once again, the decision angered people who felt that the permanence of a family was what mattered, while those who felt that biology was most important were delighted.

Not all court decisions have been decided in favor of biological fathers. In one New York case settled in 1992, a man sued to undo the adoption of a child he had fathered eighteen months before. Like Schmidt and Kirchner, he had only just discovered that there even *was* a child. But the New York court ruled that too much time had passed. The judge decided it would be too disruptive to the child to change homes at that point in his life. And in 1993, a

Baby Richard clings to his adoptive mother as she prepares to hand him over to Otakar Kirchner, his biological father.

Vermont judge settled a similar case with an unusual arrangement in which the adoptive mother and biological father were legally named the parents. The child would live with his adoptive parents, and broad visitation rights would be given to the biological father. "Nobody lost," the adoptive father said after the ruling. "The baby won."

Changes in the laws

Baby Richard cries out for his adoptive mother as his biological father tries to comfort him. The court decision, which granted custody rights to the biological father, caused enormous public controversy.

Twenty-five years ago, cases like these would not have been possible. Until the early 1970s, biological fathers had no rights at all. A man could establish a parental right only by marrying the child's mother and supporting the child. Linda Cannon Burgess, who ran an adoption agency in Washington, remembers an unmarried man who desperately wanted custody of his child. The biological mother, though, was strongly in favor of adoption. Current law did not recognize the man as the father, so he had no legal argument. In the end, he decided not to pursue the case, and the baby was adopted.

But over the years, things have changed. Fathers in society in general spend more time with their children, and some biological fathers, even unmarried fathers, are demanding more of a say in their children's care. Single fathers are becoming more common. For women who do not want to raise a child today, letting a boyfriend take custody is a legitimate option. The birth fathers of Baby Richard and Baby Jessica both reconciled with the mothers of their children, but not all men follow this pattern. More and more men are willing to consider the idea of caring for a child themselves.

Of course, even today "more and more" amounts to very few. Though most states have revised adoption laws to recognize the rights of biological fathers, by most estimates, less than one in a hundred adoptions is contested by a father who wants custody. Adoption workers would be delighted to see more involvement by birth fathers; unfortunately, most men are uninterested. According to Mary Beth Style of the advocacy group National Council for Adoption, the most common problem is birth fathers wanting out, not in. "Most of the time we can't find these guys," Style said during the Baby Jessica case.

Finding "these guys" can be very difficult—but it can be critically important. An unwilling father can derail the whole adoption process. Biological fathers who never officially give up their rights create a cloud of uncertainty around the child. When fathers are unknown, or when they disappear, it is impossible to get them to sign consent forms to allow the baby to be adopted. And without an official consent form, it can be very difficult to release a child for adoption.

A risky strategy

To avoid this kind of problem, Linda Cannon Burgess has tracked down fathers in such distant places as Turkey, Korea, Zambia, and Argentina to get them to sign release forms. When no father can be found, it is sometimes possible to proceed as if he had agreed to the adoption, but this is a risky strategy. There is always the chance that the biological father will appear some time later and demand the child. As a result, some adoption agencies no longer accept children whose fathers cannot be positively identified and located. Even when officials go to great lengths to track down a missing father, a judge may decide they did not look hard enough. In the Baby Richard case, Justice Heiple questioned whether the adoptive parents had tried their best to locate Otakar Kirchner before going ahead with the adoption. Parents who adopt a child without official consent risk putting the child at the center of a legal battle in the future.

The fathers' rights debate focuses mainly on biological fathers who do want their children. How can their rights be balanced with the needs of their children—and the

ADOPTIVE FAMILY LIFE

Among adopted teens . . .

▶ **83%** say their parents often tell them they love them.

▶ **80%** agree that each family member has at least some say in major family decisions.

▶ **75%** say they get along with their parents.

▶ **74%** say they really get along well in their families.

▶ **72%** agree that their families have "all the qualities I've always wanted in a family."

Source: *Adoptive Families*, July/August 1994.

rights of adoptive families? Today most people agree that a biological father who wants to keep his baby should be allowed to, though a few biological mothers and adoption workers express concern that an uninterested but vengeful father might block an adoption out of spite. But what happens when a father shows up after adoption proceedings have begun? Or what if he has a history of child abuse or abandonment? People disagree, often vehemently, about questions such as these.

Confusion in the law

Nearly everyone agrees on one point: The laws are a mess. Almost no two states have exactly the same policies regarding biological fathers. In an adoption that overlaps two states, such as Baby Jessica's, different courts can be expected to give different rulings. Iowa, for instance, had an unusually clear law favoring biological fathers. As the Iowa judge pointed out, the only question he could legally consider was whether Dan Schmidt's rights had been violated. In Iowa, Schmidt could conceivably have won the battle for Baby Jessica even if she had been Teenager Jessica by the time he realized that he had a daughter. California is another state where birth fathers' rights are strongly considered in adoption cases.

In other states, however, laws supporting biological parents are much weaker. The DeBoers tried to get Michigan courts to hear the case partly because Michigan law, unlike Iowa's, allows judges to consider the best interest of the child. In Nebraska, an unmarried father has precisely five days from the baby's birth to claim the child, or he loses all rights. In Minnesota, biological fathers must be notified of a pending adoption—but notification can be as simple as placing an ad in a legal journal read by virtually no one. In New York, biological fathers have lost cases that they probably would have won in several other states. This crazy quilt of adoption laws causes headaches, delays, and legal maneuvering that is clearly not in the child's interest.

Another widely recognized problem is how slowly cases move through the courts. A few months are a lifetime to a baby. "The courts should be roundly condemned for a system that allows such delays," says Howard Davidson, a lawyer whose special interest is in how the law

After a two-year custody battle, a lawyer removes two-and-a-half-year-old Jessica from the home of her adoptive parents. Critics complain that the courts take too long to reach decisions in custody cases, causing even further harm to the children.

affects children. The legal system can be compared to a ladder, with cases moving very slowly, rung by rung, from one court to the next. At each step, the loser can choose to appeal, or challenge, the last decision.

The system is supposed to ensure justice, but it is not set up for children who grow from infants to toddlers to preschoolers before cases are decided. Who rears the child while the lawyers argue and the judges deliberate? Whoever has the child has the obvious advantage of the child's steadily growing used to them as parents. The Baby Richard case might not have been so controversial if the decision had been handed down when Richard was three and a half months rather than three and a half years old. Instead, the case dragged on for more than three years—more than enough time for Richard to bond with his adoptive parents and to be aware of the changes that were taking place in his life.

Even cases that move along quickly take more time than most observers would like. The Vermont youngster whose birth father was given visitation rights was already nine months old by the time the decision was made. This case, however, was considered unusually speedy. Most proposals for reform urge that the legal process be shortened. After the Baby Richard case, for instance, the Illinois legislature passed a law that would do exactly that.

New proposals

There is general agreement that new policies are needed to deal with fathers' rights. Various suggestions include the National Council for Adoption's proposal of a so-called fathers' registry, designed to help a man who loses track of a girlfriend whom he thinks he may have impregnated. If he wants custody of the baby, he provides social service agencies with information about himself, his girlfriend, and the approximate date of the birth. If the woman has a baby around the right time and chooses to give it up, he can then step in and ask for custody, whether she tells him of the birth or not.

Five-year-old Danny Kirchner, subject of the Baby Richard court case, smiles as he holds his baby sister one year after he was placed in his biological father's custody. The lengthy Baby Richard case prompted the Illinois legislature to pass a law ensuring speedier decisions in future adoption cases.

But this solution does not satisfy everyone. Fathers' registries have been established in about a dozen states, but to date they work on a statewide level only. A nationwide project is feasible but would be much more complicated to coordinate. And a woman who lies about the father's identity—as Cara Clausen did—can make it very difficult for the registry to match father and child. In a few cases, birth mothers deliberately leave the state to give birth and then place children for adoption in foreign countries, all so the biological fathers cannot get them. Clearly, a fathers' registry is of no help here.

One social welfare group has proposed a law that gives birth fathers one month to object if a child is placed for adoption. Under this proposal, however, simply coming forward would not qualify the father for custody. First he would have to prove that he would be a good parent. Convicted criminals might have trouble with this qualification; so might a man like Dan Schmidt, who had not paid child support for his two older children.

The same proposal imposes a strict time limit on finding unknown or missing fathers. An adoption could be delayed for at most six months while authorities searched. Men who did not come forward within that time would lose all their rights. After that, though a birth father could sue an adoption agency or a birth mother if he believed they had lied, or not made every effort to find him, he could not undo the adoption or get the child back.

These suggestions make sense to many adoption advocates. "People don't trust the permanence of adoption anymore," Mary Beth Style says. Laws such as these would remove the possibility of a father's appearing out of nowhere, years after an adoption was finalized, and demanding custody. But others object to the suggestion that fathers should have to prove their ability to be parents. No one runs an automatic "parenting check" on biological mothers when babies are born, they argue; so no special rules should apply to biological fathers.

OHMAN–THE OREGONIAN. Reprinted by permission: Tribune Media Services.

More troubling to some, all of these proposals assume that at some point a biological father's rights can be terminated. Not everyone buys this argument. Ann Sullivan, director of adoption programs at the Child Welfare League, is one who wonders whether time limits on rights are constitutional. Some people argue that biological fathers should never be completely out of the picture. According to Concerned United Birthparents, birth fathers who do not officially waive their rights should be able to get their children back at any time.

Compromises like the visitation plan ordered in Vermont could be a promising solution, but compromises like this are unlikely to satisfy everybody. Some activists claim that fathers should have no rights whatsoever after an adoption has taken place. According to this argument, even limited visits are inappropriate. Activists on the other side call visitation rights a crumb thrown to men who deserve complete custody. Also, visits will work only if both sides get along. Indeed, after the Baby Jessica case, a couple in Kansas offered to pay all the Schmidts' legal fees, if they would permit the DeBoers to visit on a regular basis. It is unclear whether the DeBoers would have wanted to continue visiting Anna; in any case, the Schmidts refused.

The issue of fathers' rights remains a complicated one. Adoption remains a state-regulated rather than federally regulated practice, and laws will inevitably vary from state to state. Luckily, cases such as Baby Richard's and Baby Jessica's are rare. However, even one legal argument over a child is too many. For the sake of all the future Jessicas and Richards out there, we can hope for clarity and agreement, as soon as possible.

2

Race

FOR MANY YEARS, transracial adoption—adoption across racial lines—was practically nonexistent. Most agencies placed children with parents who resembled them in as many details as possible, attempting to match not only skin color but religion and ethnicity as well. Thus, Jewish children would be offered only to Jewish families, and a light-skinned northern European family would rarely be permitted to adopt a darker-skinned southern European child.

During the 1960s, however, this situation began to change. The number of healthy white babies available for adoption started to decrease. Easier access to birth control and abortion played a part; so did a gradual loosening of the stigma against unwed motherhood. At the same time, the number of black children entering the foster care system shot up. Some white families who were interested in adoption were unable to find children who were racial and ethnic matches. A few gave up the search, but others questioned the unavailability of black children. Yet other white families requested black children over white ones, hoping to repair the damage of decades of racism or driven by a desire to help children who needed help most. Many social workers were sympathetic to these requests. To them, it seemed that placing black children with white families was a good solution. The children got secure homes and families. The white couples were able to adopt. To many adoption professionals, adoption of black children by white families looked like an option that benefited both children and adoptive couples.

Transracial adoption rates grew slowly but steadily throughout the 1960s. By 1972, more than three thousand black children were being adopted each year by white families. This was only a handful of all the children available for adoption, but many more than had been adopted transracially ten or twenty years earlier. However, 1972 marked the high point of transracial adoption. During that year, an organization called the National Association of Black Social Workers (NABSW) issued a statement that essentially ended the practice.

The NABSW firmly rejected claims that transracial adoption helped black children. The group's opposition was on several levels. At its core was a charge that transracial adoption was an attempt by white families to "raise black children with white minds." NABSW members

A 1967 photo shows a couple with their seven adopted children and one biological child. While transracial adoption rates increased during the 1960s, they began to receive criticism during the next decade, with critics claiming that children reared by parents of another race would never gain a sense of racial identity.

doubted that any white parent could give black children a sense of racial identity. Thus, black children adopted by white families would never know exactly who they were. "Black children in white homes," said the policy statement, "are cut off from the healthy development of themselves as Black people."

The NABSW urged that social welfare agencies help preserve black families rather than simply removing children and putting them up for adoption. The group also wanted agencies to work harder to find black adoptive families. But they flatly rejected the notion that a black child was not harmed by being adopted into a white family.

The NABSW was a very small organization, but its influence was huge. The number of transracial adoptions nose-dived. The year after the statement was issued, approximately fifteen hundred black children were adopted by whites—half the previous year's total. Three years later, the figure was down to eight hundred. One by one, agencies adopted policies that made placing black children in white homes extremely difficult, if not impossible. As of 1994, forty-three states had official or unofficial rules against interracial adoptions. Nearly half of private agencies who placed children for adoption had similar restrictions. Many whites seeking to adopt are routinely told that they will not be given black children "under any circumstances." And for most of the twenty-five years since the NABSW's statement, these policies went unchallenged.

Challenges to the NABSW policy

That is no longer true. Several events and trends since 1989 have raised the issue again among many people involved in adoption. Some of these people are white foster parents who want to adopt black children in their care. Others are politicians, social workers, and psychologists. Few believe that race should never play a role in adoption, but most believe, as one activist put it, that "any home is better than no home." And they all believe that the policies shaped by the NABSW are too broad and are hurting the black children they are designed to protect.

The number of children in foster care has risen sharply over the last few years. Activists who support transracial adoption point out that a high percentage of these children are black. Though blacks make up only about 15 percent of the total population, there are at least as many black children waiting to be adopted as there are white children. For all these children to be adopted by black families, blacks would have to adopt much more frequently than whites— five times more often, according to one study. Most analysts agree that black families do not adopt at this high a rate. Indeed, a 1993 study of the California foster care system showed almost the reverse: White children were three times more likely to be adopted than black children. "It takes years longer for a black child to find a family than it does a white child," says one advocate.

Advocates of transracial adoption assert that children should be adopted into loving homes regardless of the adoptive parents' race.

If black families are not available, why not seek white families? Increasingly, activists are raising this question. Although some white families considering adoption would not choose to adopt a black child, many others say they would consider adopting a black child if one were available. One study found that white families are actually more willing to adopt older black children than black families are.

Without transracial adoption, activists argue, too many black children will never be placed with a family. "Leaving African American kids in foster care rather than allowing them to be adopted by loving parents," says one observer, "inflicts very serious harm on children." In a newspaper column, First Lady Hillary Clinton agrees: "Skin color," she writes, should not "outweigh the more important gift of love that adoptive parents want to offer."

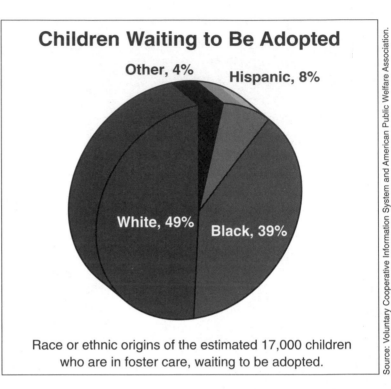

Children Waiting to Be Adopted

Other, 4%   Hispanic, 8%

White, 49%   Black, 39%

Race or ethnic origins of the estimated 17,000 children
who are in foster care, waiting to be adopted.

Source: Voluntary Cooperative Information System and American Public Welfare Association.

The case for interracial adoption has been strengthened
in recent years, too, by studies of black children who were
adopted by white families and have reached adulthood
now. Not every study has reached exactly the same con-
clusion, but nearly all agree that transracially adopted
children become happy and content adults. According to
one study, about half of minority children adopted by
whites say that race is an unimportant factor in their lives.

Arguments for transracial adoption

Many of these children say that their white parents were
very sensitive to cultural issues, as well. "Far from prac-
ticing 'cultural genocide,'" one woman writes, her family
turned out to be "sympathetic and helpful" when she
wanted to explore her racial and ethnic heritage. Another
woman believes that her upbringing helped her be "bilin-
gual" where race was concerned, able to connect with
both blacks and whites. And other transracially adopted
children feel that, if anything, white parents go too far in

emphasizing African American culture. "Not every dinner conversation has to be a lesson in black history," one study respondent complained.

Activists have pointed out, too, that "black culture" is a slippery term. "I would guess that someone like Jesse Jackson would raise a black child far differently than someone like Clarence Thomas," says black law professor Randall Kennedy. "There is no racially correct way to raise any child." Another observer argues that American blacks are simply too diverse for the phrase "black culture" to make sense. "We may not . . . dress like children who live in the ghetto," says one adult who had been transracially adopted as a child, "but that doesn't make us any less black."

Finally, advocates of transracial adoption have been disturbed by the outcome of several recent court battles. In a well-publicized 1989 case, a black boy named Reecie West was raised from the age of two months by Dale and Jan May, a white foster couple in Cincinnati, Ohio. When Reecie was freed for adoption, the Mays applied to adopt him. However, the social service department decided to search the country for a black family instead. At the last moment, the Mays' application was denied. The boy, age two and a half, was placed with a black couple in another state. Eight weeks later the boy was dead, the victim of what one report called "horrific physical abuse" at the hands of his new adoptive parents. "They didn't look at that little individual," Dale May complains about the agency. "They looked at . . . skin color and zap—that simple."

A flawed policy

Though the tragic outcome of Reecie West's case is extremely rare, the basic scenario is not. In 1992 a white Pennsylvania couple, Debi and Bill Fell, took in a biracial foster child named Michael. The Fells applied to adopt him, but their application was held up while the county social services department searched for a willing black family. A full year went by; only then did the county give up the search and allow the Fells to adopt Michael.

The following year, the Fells tried to adopt a two-year-old black girl named Alexa, who had lived with them since the age of four months. This time, their application was denied. Instead, the county ruled that a black woman named Darlene Herring should adopt Alexa instead. Though the county insisted that the decision was not about race, the Fells and their supporters believed otherwise. The Fells brought suit. They discovered that the county routinely told foster parents when children in their care became eligible for adoption—unless children were of different races from the foster parents. Two independent psychiatrists recommended that the Fells get custody of Alexa because of her "deeper bonding" with them. Nevertheless, the judge rejected the psychiatrists' report; Herring won the case.

A mother braids her adopted daughter's hair as her son looks on. While it is getting easier for parents to adopt a child of a different race, the number of recent transracial adoption court cases indicates that difficulties still exist.

The Fells were not unique. In 1992 San Francisco authorities tried to block the adoption of a black girl by the white foster parents who had raised her since she was three days old. There was no black family waiting to adopt the child; nevertheless, the county was concerned because the child's race did not match the foster parents' race. This time, the white family won their case. The adoptive father calls San Francisco's actions "the ultimate in ironies for this racially diverse and liberal city."

There have been similar cases in many other places, even in the few states where racial matching is against the law. Many people find cases like these difficult to justify. "If you are a good parent," says a Maryland woman struggling to adopt her black foster child, "it doesn't matter what color the child is." And the director of the Minnesota chapter of an African American organization agrees. "The test should be the best available family," he said in a televised interview. "Not the best available black family."

Proposed reforms

All these factors have led to increasing pressure on agencies and governments to allow more transracial adoptions. At the very least, activists argue, white foster parents should be given first crack at adopting children in their care, whatever their race. And if no black family can be found, they add, it is in the child's best interest to be placed with a family regardless of race. Other activists would like to make adoption completely color-blind. One proposed law (drafted in part by Randall Kennedy, the black law professor) would make it illegal to consider race at all in placements. The next available child would be placed with the next family on the waiting list, regardless of race. Another recent bill, the so-called Multiethnic Placement Act, tried to cut down on delays that result from searching for black families when white families are interested in adopting children.

But these proposals have had little impact. As a result of lawsuits, some agencies and governments have relaxed their rules. Illinois, among a few other states, has passed laws to make interracial adoption easier. But enforcement of these new laws is spotty. "They've just gone undercover in their placement," Reecie West's foster mother says about her county social service department. In her view, the department continues to match foster and adoptive children with parents of the same race, but will not admit it.

And in fact most states have been moving in the opposite direction. Recently, for instance, both Minnesota and California passed bills that allowed transracial adoption only as an absolute last resort. With minor changes, the stance of the NABSW today is exactly the same as it was in 1972. And many politicians, social workers, and psychologists—most but not all of them black—support the NABSW's position.

The case against transracial adoption

As it did in 1972, much of their argument focuses on cultural issues. "People don't recognize that children who have been adopted grieve the loss of their biological families throughout life," says the NABSW's Leora Neal. "A transracially adopted kid has another loss added to that—the loss of his cultural heritage and identity." Even the most well meaning whites, she maintains, cannot do an adequate job of preparing a black child for life in a white society. "White parents aren't equipped to teach a child how to deal with racism," Neal adds, "because they've never experienced it themselves." Nor does everyone accept the argument that race does not matter when a child is truly loved. "As much as the white parents may love the child," says a professor of African American studies, "the reality is, we live in a racially polarized society."

Moreover, opponents of transracial adoption suggest that most white parents never try to give their black children a sense of racial identity. Instead, they say, many white parents simply ignore the child's race. Darlene Herring, the black woman who eventually adopted Alexa, says that Alexa's hair was often tangled and unkempt when she lived with Bill and Debi Fell. "The Fells didn't seem to understand or care to learn how to groom a black child's hair," Herring says. "It seemed symbolic of a sort of basic disregard about her racial difference from them."

Even supporters of transracial adoption agree that white adoptive families need to be more in tune with the problems of being black in America. "It's of no service to the child to be color-blind," says a white adoptive mother from New York. "We don't begin to realize how deeply racism affects people in our society." But many black adoption professionals state their concerns more bluntly. "That kid is my kid," one social worker said recently about an African American boy freed for adoption in her state. "Those children belong to me. I am their past; they are my future." Black children belong with black people: For many observers, this statement is at the root of their opposition to transracial adoption.

Some opponents challenge studies that indicate that transracially adopted children are happy. Even the most enthusiastic studies recognize that some adoptees struggle with identity questions. "To the white world I was black,"

says David Watts, adopted by a white family at age two. "Yet, many blacks said I acted white." Today, Watts is an opponent of transracial adoption. Other adoptees believe that their white parents were unable to prepare them for racial prejudice, or, echoing Darlene Herring's complaint about the Fells, that they were insensitive.

Furthermore, some researchers suggest that even people who seem to have done well in transracial adoptions have hidden scars. Although white parents may make every effort to instill a sense of black identity in their adopted children, the children too often struggle with basic questions of identity. In the words of one researcher, they are "psychologically marginal" adults. "They grow up denying that they are a member of any particular racial group," says Robert Carter, a professor who has studied transracially adopted people, "and there is a consequence."

Opponents of transracial adoption interpret studies somewhat differently, as well. Too often, the research confirms their worst fear, that black children somehow lose their "blackness" if raised by white families. To supporters of transracial adoption, it is good news that half of adoptees consider race unimportant. The NABSW, however, calls

A single mother shares a playful moment with her adopted Puerto Rican daughter. Opponents of transracial adoptions claim that children with parents of another race will have a life-long struggle with their racial identity.

Adopted brothers listen attentively as their father reads a bedtime story. Critics of trans-racial adoption fear that black children will lose their "blackness" when raised by white parents.

this attitude "inappropriate." Thus, the same evidence can be viewed in two different ways. One group sees it as proof that these black children raised by whites have moved beyond race. The other side sees it as proof that cross-race adoption robs children of their racial identity.

Black families and adoption

Some adoption professionals say it is a myth that black families are uninterested in adoption. According to Robert Hill, former director of research for the National Urban League, there are about three million black families who might consider adoption, several dozen for every adoptable black child today. "We've been led to believe that there are an insufficient number of black families to adopt our children," Hill says, "and the data just doesn't support that." Other studies suggest that blacks do, in fact, adopt more frequently than whites. African Americans, one observer writes, "have the highest rate of adoption among all ethnic groups in the country."

The problem, these observers say, is that blacks are not encouraged to adopt. Rather than give up on attracting black adoptive parents, they argue, agencies need to expand their efforts. One problem that black families face is money. "Because African Americans, on average, earn less than Caucasian Americans," a professor writes, "they are less likely to be able to afford the high cost of formal adoption." And some blacks are concerned about the money issue for another reason: to them, it feels uncomfortably like the slavery system of buying and selling human beings.

Another factor masking the true rate of black adoption is the frequency of informal adoption within the black community. In informal adoption, children whose parents are temporarily or permanently unable to care for them may stay with other families—sometimes relatives, sometimes not—for weeks and months at a time before returning home, all without the government's getting involved. Most sources agree that this unofficial arrangement is especially common within black communities. As a result, some African American families may be unwilling to put up with the slow pace and specific requirements of formal adoption.

During a high school graduation ceremony, a proud father walks with his son. Supporters of transracial adoption believe that these children will grow up able to look beyond racial differences.

Finally, traditional adoption requirements have often worked against black families. Some agencies, for instance, ask that a parent stay home full-time with the child, not always an option for poorer couples, who include a disproportionate number of black families seeking to adopt. "When an African American family approaches an adoption agency to pursue a formal adoption," an agency director laments, "it is often turned away by social workers with middle-class white values." The problem is not that black families will not adopt, these critics say. It is, instead, that not enough has been done to let them.

Native American children and adoption

The debate over transracial adoption also concerns Native American children adopted by whites. Native American adoptions are subject to laws much stronger and more sweeping than the laws and policies governing the adoption of black children. These laws are based on the relatively small numbers of Native Americans in the United States and the damage done to their cultures over the last several centuries; they also seek to undo years of policies that removed Native American children from their families and tribes and placed them in white families instead. According to the Indian Child Welfare Act, a 1978 federal law, children of Native American descent are not supposed to be adopted by outsiders; indeed, in most cases they are not even supposed to be in foster care with outsiders. "Your children are the tribe," says a California woman of Pomo ancestry, locked in a custody battle for her biological grandchildren, who were placed for adoption without her knowledge. With many Indian cultures fragmented or disappearing, these laws were passed to help make sure that a Native American group's biological children would be raised as part of that group.

But some observers doubt that the laws serve their intended purpose. In a few cases, children have been taken from non–Native American adoptive parents and given to families with very little awareness of traditional ways of life. "We aren't talking about a birth father who had a connection with his culture," says one white man whose adoption of twin Indian girls was contested by the girls' part-Indian father. "This is not a Native American family unit." In other cases, Native American children have been taken at the last minute from prospective white adoptive families, only to be placed in foster care, due to a shortage of Native American families interested in adoption. Ironically, some of the foster parents are white. In Southern California, for instance, only about half the Indian children who need homes are placed with Native American families.

There is debate, too, over how much Indian ancestry qualifies children to be considered under this law. William

Pierce of the National Council for Adoption believes the minimum ought to be 50 percent. Others argue that children are Indian with as little as one-eighth Native American ancestry. The situation is even more complicated when a biological mother identifies herself as white and does not mention, or is not aware, that the father is Indian until an adoption is already in progress. In one such case, the adopted children were of less than half Native American ancestry; the biological grandmother who tried to get them back after learning of the adoption was herself only half Indian and was married to a white man.

Acts of Congress

No attempt to pass laws regarding transracial adoption has pleased everyone. Some attempts have failed to please anyone. The chief sponsor of the Multiethnic Placement Act, former Ohio senator Howard Metzenbaum, was actually disappointed when his bill passed. It had been so altered by amendments that it said something very different from what he had intended. "Agencies may not delay placement of a child" based on racial considerations, Metzenbaum had written. But by the time the bill passed, the wording had been changed to "Agencies may not *unduly* delay" (emphasis added).

The term "unduly," meaning without good reason, can be interpreted in several ways. "To many social workers who oppose transracial adoption," one magazine points out, "two months, six months, even two years is not an undue delay." Transracial adoption supporter Randall Kennedy takes the opposite position. "To a child," he says, "a delay of one day is an undue delay." In the end, the new law did nothing to clarify the controversy.

More recently, Kentucky representative Jim Bunning introduced a bill that would make it illegal for agencies receiving federal money to base placement decisions on race. Though this proposal ran into no serious opposition, it was attached to a much more controversial welfare reform bill that was vetoed by President Bill Clinton. Bunning hopes to try again.

But it is unlikely that any new law will stop debate on this issue. Supporters of transracial adoption view race as less important than matching families with kids who need them. Because permanent homes are better than foster care, they reason, getting adoptable children into good homes is essential. If that means a white home for a black child, then so be it. Opponents of adoption across racial lines, on the other hand, see race as an essential part of the whole child. When ties to racial identity are broken, the result can only harm the child. Thus, black children must be raised in black families, even if that policy means that some black children will never be adopted. The argument about transracial adoption reflects debates about race itself. Until those debates are settled, we should not expect agreement on transracial adoption.

3

International Adoption

WHILE TRANSRACIAL ADOPTION has declined over the last twenty-five years, adoption of foreign children by Americans has increased. In 1967, fewer than two thousand children from other nations were adopted into American families. In recent years the average figure has been closer to eight thousand, and the total has at times topped ten thousand. The United States is one of several wealthy Western nations that accept many foreign-born adoptees; others include Canada, Australia, Sweden, and Great Britain.

In all these countries, people who support international adoption see it as a way to make the world a better place. At its best, international adoption saves children from misery or even death. One man who adopted two Third World children says that his greatest accomplishment is "to have saved two lives—I mean that literally." But others believe that international adoption is arrogance. In their view, the practice is damaging to children and riddled with fraud and deceit.

International adoption is a complicated business. Nearly all the children adopted from abroad are born in poor nations in Asia, Eastern Europe, or Latin America. But few countries remain suppliers of children for long. New governments come to power, new social conditions require new policies; a country that allows the adoption of a thousand children one year may refuse to release any for adoption the next. In 1987, South Korean–born children accounted for about three of every five international adoptions in the United States. Not long afterwards, Korean children were almost unavailable. At various times, countries ranging from Romania to China and from India to Guatemala have been prime sources of children for adoption. One magazine coined the phrase "countries-of-the-month" to describe nations where the supply of adoptable children is large.

Because each "donor" country sets its own rules, international adoption can be confusing. Some nations have a very structured, rigorous process for adoption. Others are far more freewheeling. Some countries set stringent guidelines for who may adopt. In 1995, for instance, Americans who wanted to adopt an Ecuadorian infant had to be childless, married, and no older than forty-five, whereas Russian infants were available to single women up to fifty-five years of age. In many nations, prospective adopters are required to spend time in the country before bringing the child home. In a few cases, such as Argentina, the residency period extends for several months. Other nations

U.S. INTERNATIONAL ADOPTIONS, 1993

SENDING COUNTRIES

EUROPE	1,522
Romania	88
Soviet Union, former	1,107
ASIA	3,163
China, mainland	330
India	342
Korea	1,765
Philippines	358
Vietnam	105
AFRICA	59
MEXICO	97
CARIBBEAN	150
CENTRAL AMERICA	878
Guatemala	512
SOUTH AMERICA	1,471
Colombia	416
Paraguay	405
Peru	230

Source: U.S. Immigration and Naturalization Service, 1994.

require no visits at all; children are put on a plane with an escort, and their new families meet them at the airport.

At times international adoption can be a quick and relatively easy process. Often, however, there are hitches and delays. A couple will be on the verge of taking a child home, only to find that there has been a change in government policy, and a formerly "open" country is now "closed." In other cases, children who were supposed to have been formally released for adoption turn out not to be adoptable. Adoptions where everything seemed to be going smoothly have been held up, sometimes for months, because a couple's marriage license was not on official embassy paper or because the baby's birth certificate listed the wrong gender. Delays like these are frustrating in any adoption. They are far more difficult to deal with when a family is already in a foreign country, or when a promised child is still unseen. "The most frustrating thing," reports a woman seeking a Vietnamese child, "was trying to deal with a process going on thousands of miles away, over which we really had no control."

Poor and needy children

Against this complex background, it is no wonder that international adoption has its share of controversies. No one doubts that some poor countries have many more children than they can adequately feed, clothe, and shelter. One 1987 report estimated that there were five million homeless and abandoned children living in India alone. Social welfare institutions there, if stretched to the breaking point, could handle perhaps one out of ten of them. Some Latin American countries are known for their populations of street children—homeless boys and girls living by their wits. And wars, famines, and sudden social and economic changes all make poor and needy people even poorer and needier.

Other more stable developing nations might have more resources but also have traditions or practices that make it impossible to care for all their children. In China, a one-child-per-family policy combined with a cultural preference for boys has meant that many girls are simply abandoned by couples who desperately want a male heir. In some countries, there may be no way for a single woman to support both herself and her child. The idea of adoption is absent from a few nations, and in others adoption is very rare. All these factors contribute to the large pool of children who are unwanted in their home countries.

For some people, the obvious solution to the problem is to send as many as possible to the West to be adopted. In international adoption, "everybody wins," says an adoption coordinator who helps couples adopt children from China. The government is rid of children it cannot care for. An adoptive family is enriched by a child. And most important of all, a child is saved from a bleak future.

Many adoptive parents defend international adoption by pointing to what one parent called "the dreadful alternative." For children whose lives in their home countries would be marginal at best, adoption seems like an especially good choice. No responsible person could wish that a child anywhere grow up without education or sufficient food, living on the streets or in a hovel. "The difference [adoption] has made for our children is profound," writes Cheri Register, the mother of two girls from Korea. "International adoption has kept some children alive, saved certain children from ostracism and abuse, and spared others a life of unrelenting poverty."

The case against international adoption

But a vocal opposition disagrees. International adoption takes poor, mostly nonwhite children and transplants them to wealthy, mostly white homes. For some Western liberals and many Third World residents, this raises disturbing racial and cultural issues. For centuries, these people point out, Western Europe and the United States have colonized developing countries and exploited their resources under the process called imperialism. Many opponents of foreign adoption feel that sending poor children to rich countries is imperialist, too, a bleeding of resources and a disregard for native cultures.

This viewpoint is not new; indeed, it came up long before foreign adoptions became popular. At an international conference on adoption in 1971, a Swedish woman remarked, "Other countries show us their trust by sending brown, black and yellow children to pinkish parents." At the time, very few foreign children were adopted in Sweden. Nevertheless, she was accused of "Caucasian cultural imperialism." A British agency director admits that international adoption is a political problem for nations with a history of imperialism. As she puts it, the West is saying to the rest of the world, "You gave us your wealth and your labor; now give us your children."

An abandoned Romanian child looks out of an orphanage window. Some people criticize Westerners' adopting foreign children, calling the practice "Caucasian cultural imperialism."

This imperialist argument is compelling for many people. Just as they question transracial adoption, some observers doubt that white American families can adequately raise children born to Korean, Indian, or Honduran parents. Others bring up the issue of whether children, especially older children, will be harmed by being separated from their culture. According to one opponent of foreign adoption, children are "whisked away in cars to arrive at strange houses full of objects they've never even imagined." Learning the ways of a new culture, down to the experience of sleeping alone in your own bedroom, can be extremely difficult.

Indeed, some nations refuse to allow any foreign adoptions at all, believing that children are their most precious resource. In this view, the child belongs to the community and to the nation. Sending children abroad is considered a violation of national pride; it also can be embarrassing for nations to admit that they cannot care

An American couple dote on their newly adopted foreign baby. As with transracial adoptions within the United States, critics of foreign adoptions believe that these children will be robbed of their cultural identity.

for all their children. Some observers call international adoption an exercise in supply and demand. Third World countries supply the children; wealthy Western couples, the demand. Seen this way, children are reduced to a product, along the lines of oil, computer chips, or wood from forests. "It is troubling to speak of children in terms usually associated with inanimate commodities," Cheri Register admits.

The role of money

The amount of money spent on foreign adoption is of concern as well. "In poor countries, $25,000 would go a long way to helping support these children in their own families," complains the director of a children's rights group. When some Americans spend that much and more to obtain just one foreign-born baby, opponents of transnational adoption argue that something is wrong. Perhaps the wealth of the West should be put into improving the welfare of all children, not just a lucky few. In the words of a Korean-born four-year-old, "Why don't the American moms and dads just send money to the Korean moms and dads so they can keep their children?"

Money is a problem in other ways, too. For citizens of poor countries without much history of adoption, the fact that Westerners are willing to pay for children is suspicious. In some countries, "people only adopt when they want a servant," explains one adoption advocate. "So they think that must be what the Americans and Europeans want these kids for." Persistent rumors circulate in many countries that the Westerners "buy" their babies to use in horrible ways: selling them as slaves, harvesting their hearts and eyes for transplants, or even hollowing them out for drug smuggling. In Guatemala, two American women were attacked by a mob accusing them of doing just that.

Related to money is the question of fraud. In 1993 a British couple paid about eight thousand dollars for a Romanian baby who was not legally free for adoption. They were arrested trying to smuggle her out of the country in the back of their car. In countries where adoption is not strictly regulated, tourists who appear prosperous are approached by young couples who offer babies for sale. In one well-publicized case, the asking price was about three thousand dollars and a car. Whether the baby was the couple's or not is anybody's guess.

Stories like these crop up around the world. A hotel in Sri Lanka was said to have a "baby farm" where foreigners could take their pick of local children, in exchange for plenty of cash. There are reports in some nations of gangs who buy babies from poor women and resell them on the black market. A few Canadian agencies are offering a new service: For a fee of a thousand dollars, adoptive families can have a DNA test given to their prospective child and its biological mother, to make sure the baby was not stolen from a hospital or an orphanage. A few countries, faced with stories of baby selling, close down their international adoption services. Others simply turn a blind eye.

In their desperation for a child, British couple Adrian and Bernadette Mooney paid thousands of dollars for a Romanian baby that wasn't available for legal adoption. They were arrested trying to smuggle the baby home and were sentenced to two years and four months in jail.

In fact, governments themselves make money off wealthy North Americans. In some nations, bribery of officials is common. Couples who take the moral high ground and do not offer bribes often go home without babies. Those who try to follow the local customs sometimes run into trouble, too. One adoptive father says of his experience in Honduras: "You never know if you should be bribing this judge or not, and you can get into trouble if you bribe the wrong judge." His wife believes that the system was designed to produce money for the country. She calls adoption a "specialized tourist industry" that benefits hotels, restaurants, interpreters, government employees, judges, and only incidentally the children as well.

The impact of foreign adoption

Does corruption always go hand in hand with international adoption? Many people believe it does. It is troubling to think a nation sees adoption as a tourist industry, a way to bring in rich Westerners with plenty of cash to spend. And it is certainly true that large amounts of money can upset a fragile economy. For instance, some observers argue that budding entrepreneurs in Third World countries are attracted to the easy money of adoption rather than taking the time to build up legitimate businesses that will be good for the country in the long term.

Moreover, a few observers argue that adoption money can destroy families. Chinese orphanages, for instance, collect a required "donation" of several thousand dollars from every Western family who adopts a Chinese child. This money is a strong incentive to place children in the West. But there is no competing incentive for orphanages to try to reunite families, or to work for adoption within China. Many people argue that developing countries are better off solving problems on their own, without the attraction of Western wealth.

According to this argument, the costs of international adoption are too high. While individual children may escape terrible conditions, the existence of adoption does not benefit the nation as a whole. Even many supporters of

Canadian women proudly hold their newly adopted Chinese children after completing the sometimes lengthy and difficult adoption process.

foreign adoption accept at least part of this reasoning. People who adopt internationally "are only trying to do good," says a reporter with two adopted children from poor countries. "They don't realize that they are actually doing a great deal of harm."

Some of the harm is that foreign adoption can work a little like a safety valve. One observer summarizes the argument this way: "By exporting the children of the poor, the government avoids coming to terms with the economic and social needs of its most powerless members." Poor families can hope that their children will have a better life if they are adopted by rich Americans. But if foreign adoption were illegal, perhaps these parents would spend more time protesting conditions at home. An adoptive father says that allowing adoption is like "lift[ing] the lid on the pressure cooker a little bit, so they don't have to face the real change that may have to happen." Adoptive parents are not changing the world, he says, "in fact, we may be deferring change."

Response of adoptive parents

Most adoptive parents of foreign-born children are well aware of these attitudes. While some reject them out of hand, others are more cautious. "I did not want to think of myself as a greedy, imperialist consumer of imported children," Cheri Register writes. Supporters of international adoption usually agree that there is a "fragile line between helping those in need and exploiting them," as one reporter put it. Many adopters say that they wish there were no need for homes for these children. Register, for instance, has called foreign adoption "a temporary and very limited solution." However, most supporters of transnational adoption believe that what is best for a nation in the long term may not be what is best for children in the short run.

To counter the cultural imperialism argument, for instance, many adoptive parents establish connections with other families with children from the same countries. "Because they are never going to meet their birth parents," says one agency director, "we need to give them as many ties to their community and to their background as we can." Week-long "culture camps" may emphasize foods and holidays of children's birth nations, or may teach some of the history and the language as well. Opponents say the camps can never fully replicate the culture. Cheri Register concedes the point but questions whether it is relevant. "These are not little Koreans living in the United States," she wrote after spending time at a camp for Korean-born children. Instead, the children were "little Americans born in Korea."

A recently adopted child plays in his new room as his American parents look on. Many American couples who adopt a foreign baby make a concerted effort to teach their child about his or her native culture.

Other parents reject the culture argument even more strongly. The father of a Latin American girl says it is meaningless for his daughter to study holidays from her birth country. "Anita doesn't remember anyone ever celebrating her birthday," he says. "One day was the same as the next for her." His daughter's cultural heritage was one of poverty and illness, not holidays that she was no longer permitted to celebrate. The adoptive father of a Korean child points out that his son got his food from garbage cans. "What's 'better off'?" he asks. And some observers go even further. In a 1988 report on foreign adoptions, an advocate named Rosemary Taylor attacked the argument that children lose their culture when adopted overseas. "Nationality or citizenship," Taylor wrote, "is a meaningless concept to a child who is dead."

Supporters of international adoption inevitably return to their primary argument. They point to the poverty, prejudice, and lack of freedom experienced by children in some countries. Advocate Elizabeth Bartholet argues that children who are not adopted are consigned to the streets or understaffed institutions. If not for adoption, another woman writes, her two children "would have remained in institutions throughout childhood," assuming they survived. Many adoptive parents have similar stories. "We can't give him a good future," a Canadian woman remembers a Peruvian child's grandmother saying to her. "You can do this for him."

Foreign adoption as a positive force

Most agencies that place foreign children in the West agree that adoption is a last resort. Generally, they say their first goal is to find relatives who can take the child. If that fails, they try to place the child with an adoptive family somewhere in that country. With very few illegal exceptions, all foreign adoptions are of children who have truly been abandoned. As a children's rights group stated in a recent report: "Children are removed from their own country *only* because they essentially have no future in that country, and no possibility of being cared for by permanent, nurturing parents."

In fact, some people involved in foreign adoptions insist that many Third World parents want adoption for their children. "Abandoning children so they will be free for adoption," says Register, "is often a painful sacrifice made on the children's behalf." Instead of letting children grow up in poverty, parents relinquish them on the slim chance they will have a better life. Elizabeth Bartholet points out that immigration from Third World countries to the United States is high and would be far higher if not for restrictive American laws. Many poor people see the West as a goal; if they cannot go there themselves, then perhaps their children can. Register says that pregnant women in developing countries increasingly work with agencies and lawyers to place their children in the West, where the children will get an education and "other advantages the mothers could never afford."

As for the issue of Western money's negative effects, some foreign adoption advocates see the issue as irrelevant. Even if it undermines a society to rescue a few children, they argue, the rescue is still worth the cost. To them, the social problems in many countries cannot be solved by money alone. Moreover, they add, not every nation uses its resources wisely. China was recently accused of neglecting many children in state-run orphanages, concentrating only on those who had a chance to be adopted by Americans. Why? "Because," wrote one observer, China simply "does not wish to pay for adequate care of the vast numbers of abandoned children." Would this change if Western money was no longer available? No, these observers insist; instead, all children would be equally neglected.

A handful of adoption advocates go even further. British-born John Davies created quite a stir in Romania a few years ago. As the head of his own adoption agency, Davies was frequently accused of baby selling. Davies denied the charges, but even his supporters admitted that he was a man who made his own rules and thumbed his nose at regulations he did not like. As Davies sees it, foreign adoption works too slowly. He believes that the process of foreign adoption, as it stands now, is "more about assert-

ing state property rights over children than about children's human rights."

To Davies, governments should not be involved in adoption. Trying to bring order to its chaotic adoption policies, the Romanian government essentially cut off all foreign adoption, leaving many babies stranded in orphanages. Davies was outraged. "Bureaucrats think they are the high priests of adoption," Davies says, "and only they can bring this sacrament to the people." In his view, Western money is actually a good thing. Despite the possibilities of corruption and of babies being bought and sold, it can speed up the pace of adoptions and get children where they need to be.

While Americans debate the issue of foreign adoption, many thousands of children adopted in just this way enter the country every year. In all likelihood, the debate will continue well into the next century. And, for better or worse, as long as there are developing nations where, as one adoptive parent puts it, "orphanages are overflowing, abandoned children sleep in the streets, and poor parents see international adoption as one of the few ways to give their children decent lives," it is likely that foreign adoption will continue.

Four American couples and their adopted foreign children pose for a group photo. Though foreign adoption continues to be a controversial issue in the United States, American families still adopt thousands of foreign children each year.

4

Who May Adopt?

BORN TO AN UNMARRIED teenage mother, Gailen Brandt lived in a succession of foster homes in Washington state before being released for adoption at age two. At age three, he was placed with a Seattle couple. Both of Gailen's new parents were well-educated professionals. The affluent couple had even gone through four years of training to be adoptive parents. Some said that Gailen Brandt was very lucky to have found a good home. But others vehemently disagreed; in their view, Gailen was an innocent victim of a bad decision by the state agency that placed him. The issue revolved around the couple who took Gailen in. Their names were Ross and Luis Lopton, and they were gay.

Gailen's biological mother, Megan Lucas, was particularly upset when she found out who was planning to adopt her son. "Living with a gay couple is not what I want for my child," Lucas said. Though she had previously admitted that she had never bonded with Gailen in their time together, she went to court to fight the adoption. Washington's Department of Social and Health Services backed the Loptons. "Gailen appears to be bonding with the parents," an official said shortly after the placement was made. "[He is] doing well." When Lucas discovered that her rights as a parent had been permanently severed, she tried a very unusual maneuver: She applied to adopt Gailen herself.

The Loptons eventually won the case, but Lucas remained unconvinced that Gailen should live with them. She insisted that her objections came not because she was

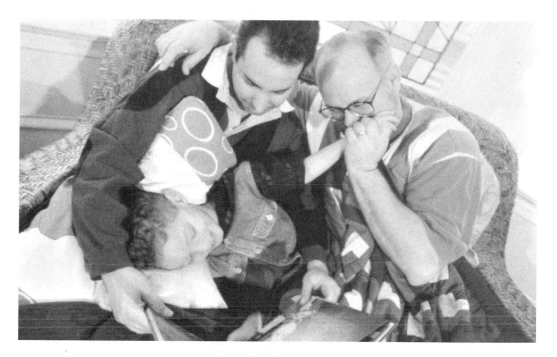

biased against gay people, but because too many other people are. "My biggest fear is the prejudice that surrounds that lifestyle," she said in an interview. "I just don't think it's very smart or very fair to put [Gailen] in that situation."

Megan Lucas is not alone. Several states have laws that forbid adoptions by gay men or lesbians. After Gailen's case became well known, several Washington legislators tried and failed to pass a similar bill in that state. And according to at least one poll, the public opposes gays as adoptive parents by about two to one. All that may mean little to Gailen and his new family, but it has a lot to say about adoptions in the future.

Who should be allowed to adopt? Many years ago, the answer to this question was easy: a healthy, heterosexual white couple, financially well off, in their late twenties or early thirties. People fitting this description were considered good parents, people who could be entrusted with the job of raising homeless infants as their own. But that was at a time when only a handful of children were considered for adoption placement. Older children, handicapped kids, and minority children were sent to orphanages or left to

Ross and Luis Lopton with their adopted son, Gailen. Gailen's biological mother fought to regain custody of her son after learning that his new adoptive parents are gay. Nontraditional adoption situations have caused many people to question who should be able to adopt children.

fend for themselves in the streets. Even fifteen or twenty years ago, healthy white children over the age of three were considered virtually unadoptable. Over the years, the pool of "adoptable" children has risen dramatically. And increasingly, agencies and social service organizations are looking at adopters who do not fit the traditional mold. Today, the answer to the question "Who may adopt?" is a lot less obvious, and a lot more controversial.

Gay and lesbian parents

Gay and lesbian adoptive parents are perhaps the clearest example of nontraditional adoption policies. A generation ago, homosexuality itself was a crime in many states. Few gays were open about their sexual preferences; fewer yet were willing to put themselves into the public eye as a couple. As gays have worked for rights, tolerance, and understanding, however, social attitudes have changed. A growing number of gay and lesbian couples has applied to adopt over the last several years. Increasingly, they are getting children, though not without a fight. "The real difficulty," says a gay activist who adopted a daughter, is the mistaken idea that "lesbians and especially gay men prey upon children."

In some states, in fact, the battleground has shifted. In New York, for instance, a state law permitted a homosexual

adult to adopt, but did not allow two legally unrelated—
that is, unmarried—gay people to adopt a child together.
Since gay marriage is illegal in New York, this meant that
only one partner in a gay couple could adopt a child. The
other had no legal standing as an adoptive parent. In 1995,
however, the state's highest court decided that unmarried
couples, including gays, could adopt together, with each
partner having full custodial rights. Gay activists, delighted
by the decision, said that the court's ruling offered a
"recognition of the integrity of gay and lesbian house-
holds." But others were displeased, on political if not moral
grounds. The state's governor, for instance, complained
that policy decisions like this were better left to the legislature, not the courts.

Agencies that accept gay adoptive parents argue that
they neither condone nor condemn homosexuality: They
are simply finding the best available family for a child. In
fact, there have been very few cases like Gailen Brandt's.
According to one estimate, only about ten children a year
are placed with gay adoptive families nationwide. When
gay parents do adopt, they are rarely given infants. More
likely, they wind up with so-called hard-to-place children
who might otherwise never be adopted—older children,
children with special needs, sometimes minority children.

Single parents

The same scenario can be applied to other nontraditional adopters. At one point, for instance, single women
had virtually no chance to adopt. This situation has so
changed that a national magazine recently ran an article ti-
tled "Single Black Women Who Adopt" and labeled it the
"latest trend in motherhood." As more people remain single, marrying later or following divorce, single men, too,
are seeking to adopt. But for many single people—male
and female alike—adoption can be a struggle.

"The ideal family still has to be a two-parent family,"
says Linda Cameron, a psychologist who herself began
thinking about adopting in 1990. In particular, many
singles complain that agencies try to steer them toward

hard-to-place children. Agencies "make you feel sort of guilty if you don't take a special-needs child or an older child," says Cameron, who eventually did adopt the baby she wanted. Another single parent agrees: "The kids that they place with single parents," she says of adoption agencies, tend to be "second-class kids."

Not all single women have this complaint. Mary Theresa Redding, for instance, had no difficulty with welfare officials in San Diego. Within three months of applying, she had a child—a baby, just as she requested. "They seemed to be surprised and impressed by my sincerity," she says. Of course, she adds, she was a bit unusual in other ways, too. "They didn't normally run into a forty-year-old federal agent driving around in a 300ZX who wanted to adopt a child," she says.

However, Redding's case is not typical. Many agencies have policies that prohibit placing infants with single parents when married couples are available. "There was no way I could adopt anything other than a fifteen-year-old with multiple disabilities," says Elizabeth Bartholet, who eventually turned to foreign adoption for the healthy babies she sought. And some agencies still refuse to allow single parents to adopt, period. Whether for practical, financial, or moral reasons, these agencies will not even consider a family that does not include two parents.

Sudden changes

What happens, though, when a two-parent family suddenly becomes a single-parent household? When Keith and Kim Lussier applied to adopt in 1993, they chose an agency that had a two-parent policy. The Lussiers were given an infant girl from Korea, whom they named Brittany. For the next five months, Brittany lived with the Lussiers. But before the adoption could be finalized, Kim Lussier died of cancer. The agency, Love the Children, called for the child's return so she could be placed with a two-parent family. The biological mother had been promised that her child would have a two-parent household, explained Mary Graves, the director of Love the

Children. "If [the biological mother] had wanted a single parent for her child," Graves argued, "she could have kept her in Korea."

Keith Lussier did not agree. Brittany had had two parents when she had come to his house, he reasoned. The child should not be moved from the only home she'd ever known just so she could have two parents. Moreover, he argued, "In the five months that she was with me, she was the happiest child anyone had ever seen." The dispute ended up in court, where a judge agreed with Lussier. "You don't just move children around because you find a better place for them," the judge said. "Maybe my kids would be better off if they were raised by the Rockefellers, but I sure hope no one takes them away from me." Despite the Lussier precedent, no doubt other cases will raise the question of whether singles should adopt, and whether they are offered the same range of children offered to couples.

Older parents

People over forty are also likely to have trouble adopting. Many agencies cut off applications at around that age; others have rules specifying that the adoptive child and parents be no more than thirty-five to forty years apart in age. These policies leave would-be older parents out in the cold, or steer them toward older, harder-to-place children. Elizabeth Bartholet felt doubly punished when she started trying to adopt. Not only was she single, but she was also already in her forties. Before Bartholet began looking for an adoptive child, she had tried reproductive technologies to overcome infertility and become pregnant. Bartholet writes with frustration about her experience: No reproductive

Many people over forty have difficulties finding agencies that will let them adopt babies. This single mother adopted her infant biracial daughter, now four, when she herself was forty.

clinics cared that she was single and over forty, but nearly every adoption agency she turned to refused to even consider her as an adoptive parent. She questions a system that permits an older single woman to use the latest scientific advances to create a baby but considers her unfit to raise a child that another woman could not care for.

Others, however, argue that age limits are appropriate. How will a child react to parents as old as some grandparents? they ask. A few critics question whether older parents have the energy to manage young children, or whether the age gap makes communication between parent and child impossible. And others point out that older people are more likely to have health problems. "I'll always remember our time together as special," writes a woman who was adopted by a fifty-year-old woman. "But she left this world much too soon for me."

Disabled parents

Other controversies about who may adopt revolve around practical limitations. Nadine and Steve Jacobson, for instance, sought to adopt a baby. They were married, well-to-do, white, and the right age. They were also blind. At one point they were just about to receive a baby boy when the lawyer handling their adoption stopped taking their calls, and the baby was given to another family instead. "The lawyer made it perfectly clear there was only one reason," Nadine Jacobson said afterwards.

The Jacobsons persisted. When they told a social worker that they would be interested in adopting a sighted child, the social worker shook her head. "I can't imagine we would even consider placing a sighted child with you," she said. Even when a blind baby came up for adoption, the Jacobsons ran into trouble. The baby was not totally blind, it turned out, and "They were worried that a partially sighted child might be too much for Steve and me," Nadine explained.

In the end, the baby was placed with the Jacobsons, but only after many years of hard work on their part. Was the process in fact unfair? Some say yes, arguing that the Jacobsons—or anyone with a disability—could nonetheless prove to be competent, caring parents. Others disagree, believing that children deserve fully able parents. In fact, Nadine Jacobson later found out that the agency was afraid that "eighteen years from now, a sighted child might sue them for forcing him to grow up with blind parents."

Adoption by parents of the same sex has caused heated debate over what constitutes a family.

What is a family?

Much of the debate over who should adopt boils down to the question of what society thinks families should look like. Some limit the definition to a traditional nuclear family structure: a relatively young man and woman, married, with a working father and stay-at-home mother. In this view, single women should not have children at all, and the concept of a family in which parents are the same sex or handicapped is discomforting. For these people, adoption adds another wrinkle to the problem. If single parenthood is to be discouraged, they contend, encouraging

Two adopted brothers walk hand-in-hand with their gay parents. Though there is much disagreement surrounding gay couples and adoption rights, homosexuals have made great strides in expanding the traditional view of the family.

single people to adopt is also a bad idea. Since gays and lesbians cannot produce babies together, they condemn an adoption system that validates them as parents, even when they are given a hard-to-place child.

But others define family much more broadly, focusing instead on the issue of finding a home for needy children. If gay couples, single women, or fifty-year-olds can care for a child, they reason, they deserve encouragement and support. If the alternative to keeping a Gailen Brandt in foster care for most of his childhood is letting him be adopted by a loving family, then the choice is simple. To supporters of nontraditional adoption, extending the definition of a family means finding children homes.

Over the last few decades, single parents, gay couples, and the disabled have gained both power and respect. They are not willing to give up their rights just to suit someone else's idea of what family means. On the other hand, traditionalists will not be pleased if increasing numbers of children go to these nontraditional families. The debate is likely to continue for many more years.

5

Who May Be Adopted?

NEARLY EVERY PUBLIC and private agency handling infant adoption has prospective parent waiting lists, some as long as ten years. There are many willing families waiting even for difficult-to-place special-needs children. One organization reports receiving fifteen hundred inquiries every year from people interested in adopting children of various ages with mental or physical handicaps. And yet, of the nearly half million children in the foster care system right now, less than 20 percent are eligible for adoption.

For most foster children, foster care is only temporary. They may be in state custody only until a father finds a job, a mother finds a home, or a long-term family illness is resolved. In fact, many foster children are placed in care with relatives or family friends. "Most children," says one advocate, "have someone else who is related to them who's usually willing to take them in." And virtually no one disagrees that short-term foster care can be a good thing, even when no relative is available.

Unfortunately, for many of these four hundred thousand children, foster care can drag on and on. "Foster care has three *R*'s," says Carol Bevan of the National Council for Adoption. "*R*emove the child, *r*ehabilitate the family, and *r*eturn the child." However, Bevan charges, "we're removing, but we don't know how to rehabilitate and we're not returning." According to one estimate, more than a hundred thousand children have been in foster care for at least the last three years. About forty thousand of them are veterans of over five years in the system.

A foster placement of three years or more is no longer temporary. To make matters worse, few of these children have one consistent foster home during this period. Some very unlucky children have had as many as ten different placements by the time they turn twelve, and Dave Thomas, the founder of Wendy's restaurant chain and an enthusiastic adoption advocate, writes of a nine-year-old boy in Chicago who had gone through seventeen foster homes.

CHILDREN WHO WAIT

The National Adoption Center prepared the following statistics based on children registered on their network as of March 22, 1991:

▶ 67% of the children are black or black/white.

▶ 52% of the children have some emotional problems.

▶ 32% of the children have some degree of learning disability.

▶ White children have more disabilities than black, with 71% having emotional problems.

▶ The largest age group is between five and eleven.

▶ The black children are younger, with 54% under eleven, compared to 31% for white children.

▶ There is a predominance of boys—almost two-thirds male.

▶ In total, 42% of the children are members of sibling groups.

▶ The average age of black children on the network is 10.2 years; white children average 12.6 years.

Source: Carole A. McKelvey and JoEllen Stevens, *Adoption Crisis: The Truth Behind Adoption and Foster Care*, 1994.

"Lost" children

Most of these long-term foster children have no real chance of being reunited with their biological families. But if biological parents do not voluntarily relinquish children, then the children can only be freed for adoption if agencies take steps to end the parents' rights to them—a difficult and time-consuming process. In 1990, for instance, welfare officials around the country identified a hundred thousand foster children who needed adoptive homes. Less than a quarter had been freed for adoption. "Kids are getting lost for a very long time," says a Michigan state representative.

Indeed, governments have to move slowly to terminate parental rights. As Carol Bevan put it, the third *R* of foster care is return to the family. The approach mandated by most governments is called family preservation: that is, trying to rebuild families so they can care properly for their children. The idea is that abusive, neglectful, or drug- or alcohol-addicted parents be given every chance to clean up their acts.

But some people believe that this approach goes too far. Especially in cases of abuse or neglect, "the state will keep kids in care for years and years and never terminate parental rights," says the National Council for Adoption's Mary Beth Style. Judy Sheindlin, a family court judge, agrees. "If the state has taken your kids because you are a drug addict," she writes, "one year is more than sufficient time to pull yourself together." As the numbers of long-term foster children show, however, such parents are often given much more than a year.

Most adoption professionals can cite from personal experience horror stories of children who have languished in the foster system. One woman forced her thirteen-year-old daughter to work as a prostitute; her other children had been removed to foster care because she had beaten them. But when a lawyer suggested that her rights be terminated, a social worker replied "I hate to give up on any mother." A California woman tied her two-year-old to an electric heater because the girl would not eat. The daughter never lived with her mother again, but the mother's rights to her were never legally cut, either. Instead, social services spent the rest of the girl's childhood trying to improve the mother's parenting skills. The girl "aged out" of the system at age eighteen—still in foster care.

Another child was removed from her drug-abusing mother ten times before she was two. "Drugs were more important to my mom than I was," she says. But she was not released for adoption; her mother insisted on keeping custody. And in another case involving a drug-addicted parent, a five-year-old who had been in foster care since birth was released to her mother's care simply because her mother attended a single Narcotics Anonymous meeting shortly before the hearing that would have terminated her rights.

Problems in the system

Adoption advocates focus attention on the problems of these children. Part of the problem, as they see it, is that social welfare agencies are overburdened and understaffed. Judy Sheindlin argues that the foster system in New York City is so complex that social workers simply cannot keep track of all the children in its care. In Iowa, all state adoption specialists recently were fired as a cost-

A foster mother poses with her adult foster children, one of whom holds her own child. Although the goal of foster care is to remove children from unsuitable parents and return them once the parents are ready to care for them, children often remain in foster care for years, sometimes moving from one foster family to another.

cutting move. In an Illinois county, eighty children due to be released for adoption had to be kept in foster care two extra months because no one had time to type up the proper court documents. As one observer wrote, moves like this "create long-term log jams of children."

Others say the problem is not lack of staff and funding, but rather the tendency of agencies to develop a close relationship over time with the biological families of children in foster care. One study concluded that these relationships make social workers reluctant to free children for adoption. And some critics point to social workers who delay severing parental ties in the perhaps false belief that the child has no chance to be adopted anyway.

A few observers argue that children are hurt because social welfare agencies have *too much* money. "Public agencies, in a sense," writes adoption advocate Conna Craig, "are paid for the number of children they prevent from being adopted." Foster children "come with tax money attached," she points out, which helps keep the system going. For special-needs kids, in particular, the federal government pays part of the cost of foster care. But once a child is adopted, the money stops coming.

This somewhat cynical view has support. One adoption official estimates that New York City agencies get five times as much money for keeping a child in foster care than they get by pursuing adoption. Another advocate claims that agencies label some kids "unadoptable" to scare adoptive parents away and keep the money coming. "All but the most persistent parents give up in the face of the 'experts,'" she complains. The problem may be worsening: A recent federal budget act sent an extra billion dollars to states to use for family preservation. "Because of the money," Carol Bevan says, states will try hard "to keep some families together that really would be better separated."

But most adoption advocates place the largest share of the blame on the family preservation approach itself. Under this system, writes one professor, foster care officials "turn adoptable two-year-olds into ravaged and virtually unadoptable seven-year-olds." Judy Sheindlin writes scathingly of "management teams" that devote years to working with abusive or neglectful parents whose children bounce from one foster household to another. And when Michigan legislators recently held hearings on adoption policies, they heard from many eager foster parents unable to adopt their foster children because of laws and policies that mandated family preservation efforts first.

Other factors

A few adoption advocates worry about the declining number of babies available to be adopted. Only a small percentage of women who consider adoption actually go through with it: Perhaps 3 percent of babies born out of wedlock in the United States are given up for adoption. "Too many social workers bend over backwards to talk women out of giving their children up for adoption," says William Pierce of the National Council for Adoption. The head of a California agency complains about counselors and social workers who believe that "only someone who doesn't love the child" would choose adoption, fearing that some of the women who are talked out of adoption will eventually consign their children to a lifetime in the foster care system.

Many studies find an inferior quality of life in children who are born to, and raised by, young single women. "In most of the cases," says George Clements, a Chicago priest, "there is no father present; the mother is so often on welfare and not able to take care of herself, let alone another human being." Perhaps, he suggests, those children are better off with another family. And a few observers believe that children, in general, are simply better off with stable middle-class families than with poor and unemployed parents. "Adoption is a powerful huge intervention that reshapes individual lives," says one psychologist.

Other advocates stress adoption as an alternative to abortion. A recent television commercial sponsored by the pro-life DeMoss Foundation encouraged young pregnant women to "tough it out" and consider adoption rather than

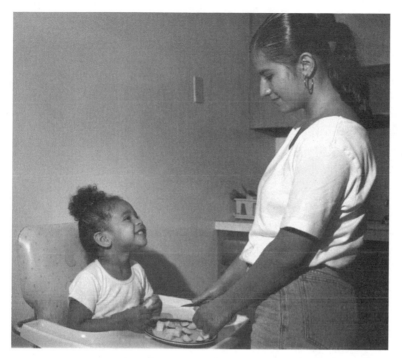

A teenage mom prepares dinner for her young daughter. While some teenagers are able to bear the hardships of mother-hood, others find it too difficult and end up placing their children in foster care.

choose abortion. Antiabortion demonstrators sometimes carry signs with messages like "Don't Throw Them Away—Give Them Away"; for them, adoption is the preferred alternative to abortion. If a young pregnant woman believes she cannot give her baby a good home, they reason, she has the choice, perhaps even the moral obligation, to bear the child and find it a good adoptive home.

Suggestions for change

Advocates for adoption have many ideas about how to change the system. They would start by shifting the emphasis from family preservation to serving the best interests of the child. Conna Craig, for instance, agrees with Judy Sheindlin that biological parents should get only one year to prove their fitness for parenting. Writes Craig, "We remind them that they really are responsible for their actions." Craig also urges that states be given a month to find homes for children who are released for adoption; if the state cannot, then it should pay a for-profit private agency to do it instead. "Because they are not paid until they place a child," Craig writes, "private agencies are good—and quick—at finding qualified families."

Other solutions hinge on local laws and on individual action. A bill in Michigan would allow foster parents to file for custody of their long-term foster children. One Florida boy successfully filed suit to "divorce" his biological mother, thus freeing himself for adoption by his foster family. In Utah, another bill would pay unmarried women if they carried their pregnancies to term and then placed the child with another family. Dave Thomas of Wendy's, responding to concerns that adoption is too costly, suggests tax credits for those who adopt; some members of Congress have suggested similar bills. And George Clements, the Chicago priest, is leading a movement to encourage blacks to adopt children stuck in the foster care system.

Opposing viewpoints

The proposals are challenged by many different people, however. Some oppose the whole institution of adoption; they fear that the institution no longer serves children, but is instead devoted to providing babies for infertile couples. Others are social workers who firmly believe that family preservation is the best way to go. Still others are child advocates who doubt that adoptive homes can actually be found for all the children now in foster care. In their eyes, there are too many, not too few, kids available for adoption.

Many feminists, in particular, are concerned about the abortion-adoption connection. The DeMoss pro-adoption commercial angered some pro-choice advocates, who argue that it is overly simplistic to tell pregnant women that an unwanted child should be carried to term and placed for adoption rather than aborted. Mary Logan, an official for Planned Parenthood, wonders how realistic adoption can be for women without much money or family support. "Regardless of how they feel about adoption," she says, "it's just simply not an option for them at that point in their lives." And another pro-choice counselor goes even further. To the extent that a woman can choose either adoption or abortion, she argues, abortion is the better choice. "Adoption is a violent act," she writes. Compared to "early, safe abortion . . . there is no contest."

Other commentators object to social workers' urging women to give up babies for adoption. Their concern is with the birth mother and the possibility that she will feel a sense of pain and mourning. Some writers, calling this feeling a "limbo loss," oppose any efforts to encourage women to relinquish children. "Birthmothers are seldom at peace," writes one advocate. Carole Anderson of Concerned United Birthparents compares people who adopt infants to people who would "take a living person's eyes" in order to see. When adoption can cause a woman such pain, the argument goes, it is immoral to ask anyone to place a baby for adoption, for any reason.

Some advocates worry about reports of stolen babies, as well. Several women have told of being forced to give up babies for adoption. Unmarried and pregnant, nineteen-year-old Krista Stoner went to a crisis pregnancy center in San Diego seeking information on her options. But when she went into labor, the staff refused to take her to the hospital until she agreed to let her baby be adopted. "You have to choose a family for your baby," she remembers the staff insisting. Immediately after birth, the baby disappeared into what one article called a "fundamentalist Christian underground adoption network." Stoner brought suit against the director of the clinic and won a judgment of $300,000—but did not get her baby back. There may be many such centers in the baby business. "Women are lured in by promises of free pregnancy tests," a reporter explains. Then, as in Stoner's case, they are "hounded at home and work" by counselors who try to get them to carry the baby to term and give it up for adoption.

"It's a baby market out there"

Another concern involves money. When domestic adoptions can cost many thousands of dollars, there may be reason to believe that poorer women are being "bought" to provide newborns for richer families. Adoption treats

children like "pricey commodities," writes Carole Anderson. Another writer refers to a "shadowy and competitive adoption bazaar." People who are not worried about this aspect of adoption should be, a few observers argue. "Feminists have been slow to recognize adoption's exploitation of their sisters," says a women's health guide. "It's a baby market out there," agrees another advocate. "You see advertisements for babies right next to ads for Volvos in the newspaper." And social worker Reuben Pannor says that money is a huge part of adoption. Baby brokers, he says, "are buying babies from married couples. They promise jobs for the husband and toys for the other kids in the family. . . . And when it's over, the poor family has to give away their baby."

This question of class exploitation also affects the way some people think about foster care. They worry that children may be taken away from poor families just because they are poor. In particular, many social workers and other advocates are not happy with the "best interests of the child" standard. "If you had a straight best interests test between most birth parents and most adoptive parents, the birth parents would lose all the time," says John Stupp of the New York State Department of Social Services. "Who are the people that have kids taken away from them?" asks a law professor. "These are poor people. . . . You see the class bias here." The lawyer who handled the Baby Jessica case for the Schmidts says that the best interests guideline would turn parenting into a "negotiable right"—a right that could be taken away by the government for any reason at all.

In defense of family preservation

Finally, supporters of family preservation argue that the current approach, while flawed, is quite workable and should not be scrapped. When family preservation works, intervention by social services means that a child is returned to the care of people who have known him or her since birth, surely the best possible outcome. And even when reuniting a family is impossible, some advocates still say that a family preservation approach makes sense. With family preservation, "you have so much better, more reliable, provable information on which to base a decision" about whether a child ought to be placed for adoption, says Mark Harmon of the American Bar Association's Center on Children and the Law.

Homeless women sit at a table with their two young children. While some critics believe that children who receive inadequate care from their parents should be placed in foster care, others contend that it is better for children to remain with their biological parents despite the circumstances.

Indeed, family preservation continues to be widely supported in the United States. Some judges will not terminate parental rights unless there is an adoptive family ready to take a child in immediately. They reason that even the dim possibility of reuniting a child with the biological parents is better than the possibility of no family at all. Many others agree. Annette Baran, for instance, says that still more work needs to be done to strengthen existing families. And some argue that what is needed is money: With more resources given to the welfare system, with more money given to family preservation, perhaps more biological parents could provide good homes for their children. Perhaps, too, the children who needed temporary foster care would get just that: temporary care.

Perhaps. The controversy over who may be adopted is central to the question of what adoption means. Americans do not yet agree whether adoption is about putting children in the best possible home, or whether adoption is about favoring the middle class at the expense of the poor. Some argue that children must remain connected to their birth parents almost no matter what; others say that cutting those ties is the greatest possible gift for some children. Social service professionals continue to debate whether our laws and policies should make adoption easier or harder. Meanwhile, children wait.

6

The Need to Know
and the
Right to Privacy

An AIR OF SECRECY has often surrounded the
adoption process, especially where infants are concerned.
Forty or fifty years ago, adoptive parents often concealed
the fact of their children's adoption. Birth mothers were
expected to sign the appropriate adoption papers and then
disappear to "get on with their lives," often without anyone besides their immediate families knowing they had
been pregnant. There was no expectation that adoptive
children would want to make contact with their birth families, or that women might wonder how their biological
children were faring.

Over the last twenty years or so, however, this pattern
has changed. It is very rare today to find adopted children,
even young ones, unaware that they are adopted. As teen
pregnancy increases, placing a child for adoption carries
less stigma than it once did. And increasingly, adoption
experts are recognizing that for at least some adopted children and birth parents the secrecy of adoption can be a
problem.

What adopted children should know about their biological parents, what birth parents should know about their
adopted children, and what adoptive parents are entitled to
know about their adopted child's medical and family
history are at the heart of the debate over secrecy and

Members of the Council for Equal Rights in Adoption rally for the right of adopted persons to know their true birth history.

openness in adoption. Is it good for birth parents to meet the children they gave up for adoption? What if one party wants contact and the other does not? As is true of many other adoption controversies, emotions on all sides run high. One adoption advocate calls legislation to lift some of the traditional rules of confidentiality "a disastrous invasion of privacy." Others disagree. According to a thirty-five-year-old adoptee looking for his biological mother, "My right to know is greater than her right to privacy."

Today, the most an adult adoptee can seek is something called "nonidentifying" information about his or her biological parents. Nearly all states now offer this service. As the name implies, this information describes biological parents without actually naming them. An adoptee might be told, for instance, what region of the country his or her biological parents lived in, what their religion was, how old they were, and perhaps their ethnic background. Because of the possibility of hereditary diseases, medical information is sometimes available, too. But in most cases this is all. Except in a very few states, original birth certificates are destroyed or irrevocably sealed when a child is adopted. The names and addresses of birth parents, in other words, are simply not available to adoptees.

Questions of identity

Many people argue that this makes no sense. According to many adoption experts, adopted children often experience a feeling of rootlessness. As one writer puts it, "a piece of their identity puzzle is missing." A biological parent can fill in some of the missing gaps. "The lives of many adoptees begin at Chapter 2," says Michael Sobol, a Canadian adoption expert. Along with many other adoption professionals, Sobol believes that there ought to be a mechanism to allow children to forge a relationship with biological parents. "Finding their birth parents," Sobol argues, "helps complete their identity."

For some adoptees, the nonidentifying information is enough. Linda Cannon Burgess writes of a woman who was eager to meet her biological parents. She first obtained nonidentifying files at the agency that handled her adoption. The files gave her a clear picture of the reasons why her biological parents had chosen adoption. When Burgess asked the woman whether she wanted to search further, she was told: "I don't think I need to anymore."

But not every adoptee feels this way. People who have searched for their biological parents speak of wanting to know more than just medical histories and educational levels. Some long to find people who look like them and identify traits inherited from birth families. Others simply want to hear family stories and get a better sense of their cultural heritage. "I love my adoptive parents," says a woman who found that her birth father was an Indian chief. "But they can't give me my own history."

Searching for biological parents, however, is complicated. Only a handful of adult adoptees—between 2 and 6 percent, by most estimates—ever mount a search. Many have no interest in finding their biological parents, but others are put off by the difficulty of searching. Because governments and agencies rarely release information, much of the search process is left to private organizations. These can be expensive as well as time-consuming; like detectives, they place ads in newspapers, comb old year-books and city directories, and spend hours tracking down leads on the phone. But there is no guarantee that biological parents can still be traced after eighteen or more years, and no guarantee that they will want to see their adult children if they are found.

Suggestions for change

In response to these difficulties, several states have established voluntary registries that can help pair adopted adults and their birth parents. These registries are open only to adults. An adult adoptee who would like to find his birth parents gives the registry his date and place of birth and any other important details. Birth parents who wish to find their biological children do the same; if information matches, the two are put in touch with each other.

Though these registries are not especially controversial, some search advocates say that they do not go far enough. For one thing, not every state has one. A national registry

---

LEARNING ABOUT BIRTH PARENTS

Among adopted teens . . .

▶ **65%** would like to meet their birth parents, but haven't.

▶ **65%** think about their birth mother once a month or less.

▶ **77%** think about their birth father once a month or less.

▶ **52%** wish they knew more about their birth mother.

▶ **45%** wish they knew more about their birth father.

▶ **1%** have met at least one birth parent.

Source: *Adoptive Families*, July/August 1994.

Advocates of adoption registries speak with New Jersey senator Wynona Lipman about implementing an adoption reform bill that would link adoptees to their birth parents.

would make more sense; a congressional bill to establish one has been proposed but not yet passed. Another drawback is lack of public awareness: Signing up for a registry is an active step, and adoptees and birth families who might like to meet cannot unless they know about the registry.

A few states have proposed a more sweeping reform. A recent law in Tennessee, for instance, gives adoptees over the age of twenty all information the state has about their birth parents, including names and addresses. Similar laws are under consideration in other states as well, including Ohio, New York, and Colorado. In some states, the proposed change is small but powerful. A birth mother would be automatically entered into the registry, unless she specifically requests that her name be kept off the list. In Tennessee, following a law passed in parts of Australia and Canada, the birth mother cannot keep her name out of the registry. However, in what is called a contact veto, she may request that her biological children not contact her. A subsequent attempt by adult adoptees to contact the birth parent is a criminal offense.

Public opinion favors such new laws. Some pro-search groups call the need to know personal histories a fundamental right. "I'm not looking for a relationship," says a Tennessee woman who was stymied in her search for her biological mother under the old law, "and I'm definitely not looking for a family. It's the unknown that gets my goat." Linda Cannon Burgess points out that the adopted child "signed no document . . . pledged no secrecy." How, she asks, can we deny them all the information they want when they reach adulthood? A handful of adoptees go as far as to refer to themselves as orphans. They regard knowing their birth parents as both healthy and necessary.

Questions of privacy

But not everyone agrees. Many observers believe these new laws violate the biological mother's privacy. "I pray to God that he doesn't come looking for me!" says a woman who gave her newborn son up for adoption twenty-four years ago. "Birth parents are often put in embarrassing, and sometimes extremely painful, situations by the unexpected arrival of an adoptee," writes political columnist Mona Charen. Many birth parents feel that they have put a painful part of their lives behind them; a phone call or a visit would reopen old wounds. "I may want to see my son someday, but I can't face it yet," says a birth mother whose child is now grown.

Indeed, William Pierce of the National Council for Adoption questions whether laws can be changed after the fact. For adoptions that involved promises of confidentiality, Pierce says, "it is illegal and unconstitutional for the state to change the rules retroactively." And some observers say that the net effect of these laws will be to turn single women away from adoption and toward abortion. "A scared young woman will not risk someone later coming and finding out what she did," says Pierce. Similarly, Mona Charen points out, when records were opened in Australia and Great Britain, the number of adoptions dropped considerably.

A New York City woman, who was adopted as a child, receives a court order allowing her to receive a copy of her original birth certificate.

Another concern about opening records involves the effect on adoptees whose biological parents do not want to see them. "I used to tell people that the hardest part of being adopted was not knowing," wrote a woman who found her birth mother, only to have contact suddenly cut off for no apparent reason. "Now I know that the hardest part is knowing." Some adoptees call the discovery that their birth parents do not want to see them a second rejection. "I think it does the child a great disservice if the parent does not want to meet," agrees a birth mother who does not want contact. Many adoptees point out that they do not feel a sense of incompleteness, and others hesitate to search, afraid of what they might find. According to one report, when Great Britain's records were opened in 1975, only about two adoptees in a hundred chose to learn their biological parents' names, and even fewer actually tried to track those parents down.

For many critics of greater openness, the contact veto is no solution, either. "The contact veto isn't much protection for people who don't read the paper," argues Carol Chumney, a Tennessee state legislator who opposes her state's new law. She worries about birth mothers who would prefer not to have information revealed but "don't know their identity could be given out if they don't do anything." Pressure from birth parents who did not want their biological children to identify them killed a proposed open-records law in the Canadian province of Alberta.

Some advocates for more open records also dislike the contact veto; they believe that nothing should stand in the way of a child who wants to know his or her heritage. The contact veto is "in praise of ignorance," writes one observer; it denies adoptees "active participation" in their lives. While support for the contact veto seems to be growing in the United States, the same is not true worldwide. In New South Wales, Australia, one of the first governments to institute the idea, the contact veto has recently been eliminated in favor of a law that requires birth parents' agreement to release any identifying information at all.

Birth parents' rights

A related debate swirls over what birth parents are entitled to know about their adopted children. Advocates for birth parents argue that they have the same sense of loss as adopted children do, and should have the right to find their children, at least once the children turn eighteen. "A spot in my heart was always empty," says one woman who gave up her daughter at birth; "I think about him every day," says another of her son. Organizations like Concerned United Birthparents have pushed for laws that will allow birth parents to make contact with their biological children.

However, these proposals are controversial. Even many supporters of open records do not believe that biological parents have the same rights as adopted children. As Linda Cannon Burgess points out, the birth mother made a choice. "The prior relinquishment of parental rights made voluntarily is forever binding," she writes. Mona Charen writes of the pain experienced by adoptees who are "sought after by birth parents they have no wish to see." Some fear that birth parents who regret their decisions will stalk children even before they reach adulthood. Indeed, several such cases have been reported, and there have been arrests of people who have used bribery or fraud to obtain information for birth mothers. Even states that have relaxed their laws have not made it easier for birth parents to get information about their children.

Open adoption

Increasing numbers of open adoptions have eliminated the need for a long and involved search. In an open adoption, the biological mother and the adoptive parents are known to each other; in some cases they meet and exchange information, and in other cases information is channeled through intermediaries. As the children grow older, exchange of information may continue. One family writes of letters, pictures, and videos sent to the birth mother through the adoption agency. In a few open adoptions, there may even be regular visits. "We came to love and admire" the birth mother, says an adoptive mother. "As a result, we keep in close touch and even visit." Open adoption eliminates the need for lengthy investigation; all the relevant information would be on file, often known from the beginning of the adoption, and easily accessible.

Evaluating the success of open adoption is difficult because the trend is still relatively new, but many birth parents are enthusiastic about the process. "I just wanted to see them," one woman says about her meeting with the couple who would adopt her baby, "to know my son would be OK." In open adoptions, birth parents are given a lot of say in who adopts their children. Having a voice may make birth parents more willing to consider adoption and less likely to regret it afterwards, since the biological parents know that the child will be well cared for.

Adoptive parents, on the other hand, are less easily convinced of the value of open adoption. Some fear that the birth mother will try to take the children back. Others worry that it will be confusing to the child to have two sets of parents. However, many agree that it makes sense. "It was important for me to know why she was giving up her baby," one adoptive mother said after talking face-to-face with her child's biological mother. And in one study of adoptive parents involved in open adoptions, the biggest concern turned out to be that the birth mother was not involved enough.

Recognizing its pitfalls, some of the system's most enthusiastic early supporters have turned away from open adoption, convinced that agencies now use it as a tool to lure birth parents to give up their children. Most promises of letters, pictures, and progress reports are verbal and cannot be enforced should adoptive parents decide to cut the biological family out. A few birth mothers have found to their dismay that what they thought would be an open adoption was not open at all. Many observers ask what-if questions: What if a birth mother demands more control over a child's upbringing? What if a birth mother pulls out suddenly, or if an adoptive family decides to cut off further contact?

Some even see open adoption as very dangerous. One writer warns that the practice will turn adoptive parents into "long-term foster caregivers" and will "lead to real disaster stories" when some of today's children grow up. To him, open adoption undercuts the role of the adoptive family. Similarly, some adoptive families question whether birth mothers should have so much power in choosing a family for their children. One couple compared their interview with a set of birth parents to the audition-

Proponents of open adoption gather during a demonstration. Those who are adopted, they argue, have the right to know the identities of their biological parents.

format television show *The Dating Game*. Others worry that the choice of adoptive parents may be based on details such as a couple's favorite food or first names, not on whether they can take excellent care of a child.

In the long run, open adoption may be a solution to the dilemma of openness and secrecy, or it may be more trouble than it's worth. For now, the debate continues. Some people seem willing to do anything to find their "missing halves"; no doubt others will go to great lengths to avoid them. One group claims a right to privacy; the other claims a right to identity. Even the best-intentioned laws involve some degree of disruption to one or more parties to adoption. Our society's task is to determine how we can best minimize that disruption while giving everyone what they need.

Glossary

adoptee: A person who has been adopted.

adoption agency: Any public or private organization that places children for adoption.

adoptive family: A family with one or more adopted children.

best interests of the child: A policy designed to consider the needs of a child before examining what is best for adoptive or biological parents.

contact veto: A provision of laws in several *open records* states and countries that forbids adoptees from contacting birth parents who have stated that they do not want contact.

family preservation: The umbrella term used by many social service organizations to characterize efforts including parenting training, temporary foster care, and rehabilitation, all aimed at keeping an original family intact.

fathers' registry: A list of men who suspect they may have impregnated a woman and who want custody of the child. Fathers' registries are typically kept by governments, who alert the men if a baby fitting the right description is born. At present, less than half the states have one.

international adoption: Also called transnational adoption. The adoption of a child of one nationality by parents who are citizens of another country. Today, this typically means the adoption of a child from parts of Asia, Latin America, or Eastern Europe by a Western European or North American family.

nonidentifying information: Information released to adult adoptees that gives the adoptee a sense of his or her background without actually giving names and addresses of birth parents.

nontraditional adopters: Adoptive parents who do not fit the traditional mold of nuclear adoptive families; in particular, they are single, disabled, older than forty, or homosexual.

open adoption: An adoption in which the identity of the birth parents is not kept secret. In some cases, there may be meetings between birth parents and adoptive parents, or even between birth parents and adopted children.

open records: A system that allows adoptees to find out information about their birth parents.

special needs: One of several terms (another is hard-to-place) used to describe a child whose medical history, racial background, or age make adoption difficult.

transracial adoption: Also called interracial adoption. The adoption of a child of one race by a family of another race. Today, this term is most often used to describe the adoption of black, biracial, or Native American children by white families.

Organizations to Contact

Adoptive Families of America
3333 Highway 100 North
Minneapolis, MN 55422
(800) 372-3300

This organization's mission is to provide services and supports to adoptive parents around the country. It advocates adoption for waiting children and puts out educational materials dealing with adoption, including the magazine *Adoptive Families*.

American Adoption Congress
1000 Connecticut Ave. NW, Suite 9
Washington, DC 20036
(202) 483-3399

This group has a particular interest in helping adult adoptees search for biological families. The organization advocates search registries and new laws; it describes itself as "dedicated to promoting openness and honesty in adoption."

Child Welfare League of America, Inc.
440 First St. NW, Suite 310
Washington, DC 20001
(202) 638-2952

This organization concerns itself with many different kinds of children's services including adoption, day care, foster care, and teen pregnancy. It describes itself as "helping deprived, neglected and abused children and their families."

Concerned United Birthparents
2000 Walker St.
Des Moines, IA 50317
(515) 263-9558

As its name implies, much of this group's membership consists of birth parents. The organization supports adoption reform, especially where open records legislation is concerned. Among its stated goals are "support for coping with the ongoing pains and problems of adoption" and "assisting adoption separated relatives in searching for family members."

National Council for Adoption
1930 17th St. NW
Washington, DC 20009
(202) 328-1200

This group considers adoption a benefit to society. It functions in part as an umbrella organization for private adoption agencies. Besides preserving confidentiality in adoption, the group works "to promote adoption as a positive option for young, single, or troubled parents."

North American Council on Adoptable Children
970 Raymond Ave., Suite 106
St. Paul, MN 55114-1149
(612) 644-3036

This group's interest is in children waiting to be adopted. It provides training and support for adoptive parents. It describes its mission as "to advocate the right of any child to a permanent, continuous and nurturing family, and to press for the legal adoptive placement of any child denied that right."

Suggestions for Further Reading

Christine Adamec and William L. Pierce, *The Encyclopedia of Adoption*. New York: Facts On File, 1991.

"All in the Family," *New Republic*, January 24, 1994.

Conna Craig, "What I Need Is a Mom," *Policy Review*, Summer 1995.

Sarah Glazer, "Adoption," *CQ Researcher*, November 26, 1993.

John D. Hull, "The Ties That Traumatize," *Time*, April 12, 1993.

Michele Ingrassia, "The Limits of Tolerance," *Newsweek*, February 14, 1994.

———, "Ordered to Surrender," *Newsweek*, February 6, 1995.

Michele Ingrassia and Karen Springen, "She's Not Baby Jessica Anymore," *Newsweek*, March 21, 1994.

———, "Standing Up for Fathers," *Newsweek*, May 3, 1993.

Ruth G. McRoy, Harold D. Grotevant, and Susan Ayers-Lopez, "Open Adoption," *Adoptive Families*, January/February 1995.

Ronnie Polaneczky, "Hearts Divided," *Redbook*, September 1995.

Cheri Register, *Are Those Kids Yours?* New York: The Free Press, 1991.

Claire Safran, "Stolen Babies," *Good Housekeeping*, March 1995.

Jill Smolowe, "Adoption in Black and White," *Time*, August 14, 1995.

Anne Swardson, "A Father's Trial," *Good Housekeeping*, June 1995.

Beth M. Waggenspeck, "Damaging Images," *Adoptive Families*, November/December 1994.

Steven Waldman and Lincoln Caplan, "The Politics of Adoption," *Newsweek*, March 21, 1994.

Works Consulted

"As Simple as Black and White," *60 Minutes*, CBS newsmagazine broadcast of October 25, 1992.

Elizabeth Bartholet, *Family Bonds: Adoption and the Politics of Parenting*. Boston: Houghton Mifflin, 1993.

Mary Katherine Benet, *The Politics of Adoption*. New York: The Free Press, 1976.

Linda Cannon Burgess, *The Art of Adoption*. Washington, DC: Acropolis Books, 1976.

Holly Burkhalter, "China's Horrific Adoption Mills," *New York Times*, January 14, 1996.

Patricia Chisholm, "A Journey of the Heart: Adult Adoptees Press Governments to Open Up Their Birth Records," *MacLean's*, November 28, 1994.

Kim Forde-Mazrui, "Black Children and Child Placement: The Best Interests of Black and Biracial Children," *Michigan Law Review*, February 1994.

Lucinda Franks, "The War for Baby Clausen," *New Yorker*, March 22, 1993.

E. Kaye Fulton, "Bringing Home Baby," *MacLean's*, August 21, 1995.

Lisa Gubernick, "How Much Is That Baby in the Window?" *Forbes*, October 14, 1991.

Karima A. Haynes, "Single Black Women Who Adopt: Latest Trend in Motherhood," *Ebony*, May 1994.

Nadine Jacobson, "Loving Elizabeth," *Family Circle*, October 10, 1995.

Bechetta A. Jackson, "Should White Families Adopt Black Children?" *Jet*, May 8, 1995.

Tom Junod, "Someone Else's Child," *Gentleman's Quarterly*, December 1994.

Ina Kichen, "Long Journey, Happy Ending: Adopting a Foreign Child," *Business Week*, June 12, 1995.

Tamar Lewin, "Tennessee Is Focus of Debate on Adoptees' Birth Records," *New York Times*, March 18, 1996.

Mary Martin Mason, "The Great Debate," *Adoptive Families*, November/December 1995.

Sherry Davis Molock, "Adoption Barriers for African-American Families," *Adoptive Families*, March/April 1995.

Marvin Olasky, "The War on Adoption," *National Review*, June 7, 1993.

Judy Sheindlin, *Don't Pee on My Leg and Tell Me It's Raining*. New York: HarperCollins, 1996.

Rita Simon, *Transracial Adoption*. New York: John Wiley and Sons, 1977.

Lynn Smith, "A Child's Place," *Los Angeles Times*, November 21, 1995.

Arthur D. Sorosky, Annette Baran, and Reuben Pannor, *The Adoption Triangle*. New York: Archer Press, 1978.

Dave Thomas, "Every Child Deserves a Family," *Family Circle*, November 21, 1995.

Charlotte Vick, "Where Kids Get Stuck in the System," *Adoptive Families*, November/December 1995.

Ruth B. Ward, "By Any Civilized Standard," *The Humanist*, September/October 1995.

Index

About the Author

Stephen Currie is the author of more than twenty books and many magazine articles. Among his nonfiction titles are *Music in the Civil War*, *Birthday a Day*, *Problem Play*, and *We Have Marched Together: The Working Children's Crusade*. He is also a first and second grade teacher. He grew up in Chicago, where he spent many hours laboriously composing stories on an ancient manual typewriter, and now lives in Poughkeepsie, New York, with his wife, Amity, and two children, Irene and Nicholas.

Picture Credits